STEPHEN TUROFF carpenter but soon focus fully on spiri years' experience, h psychic therapists i the Power of Light to raise consciousness, bring inner balance and well-being. Stephen is also a teacher of meditation and kriya yoga and holds seminars which lead to a deeper understanding of who we are as human beings and the purpose of our life in this world. Based in Essex, England, Stephen continues to help numerous individuals with their personal development and healing, both in the UK and abroad.

STEPPING INTO ETERNITY

A CONVERSATION ON THE AFTERLIFE

STEPHEN TUROFF

Clairview Books Ltd.,
Russet, Sandy Lane,
West Hoathly,
W. Sussex RH19 4QQ

www.clairviewbooks.com

Published by Clairview Books 2025

© Stephen Turoff 2025

This book is copyright under the Berne Convention. All rights reserved. Apart from any fair dealing for the purpose of private study, research, criticism or review, no part of this publication may be reproduced, stored in a retrieval system, or transmitted in any form or by any means, electronic, electrical, chemical, mechanical, optical, photocopying, recording or otherwise, without the prior written permission of the copyright owner. Inquiries should be addressed to the Publishers

No part of this book may be used or reproduced in any manner for the purpose of training artificial intelligence technologies or systems. In accordance with Article 4(3) of the DSM Directive 2019/790, Clairview Books expresssly reserves this work from the text and data mining exception

The right of Stephen Turoff to be identified as the author of this work has been asserted in accordance with sections 77 and 78 of the Copyright, Designs and Patents Act, 1988

A CIP catalogue record for this book is available from the British Library

Print book ISBN 978 1 912992 75 1
Ebook ISBN 978 1 912992 76 8

Cover by Morgan Creative
Typeset by DP Photosetting, Neath, West Glamorgan
Printed and bound by 4Edge Ltd, Essex

Contents

Preface 1

1. It Begins 3
2. Karma, Cause and Effect 10
3. Meeting my Spiritual Guide 24
4. Out of the Darkness 37
5. Embrace of Heaven 47
6. New Beginnings 66
7. The Frequencies of Life 85
8. Relationships 99
9. Ghostly Impressions 120
10. Dreams 140
11. The Summons 156
12. The Medium of Music 167
13. The Battle 176
14. Chan's Gift to Jim 188

Preface

It's been thirty years since I wrote *Seven Steps to Eternity*. I recall vividly the emotions and thoughts that filled my mind as I recorded the tale of a young soldier who met his untimely end in the horrific Battle of the Somme during World War I. In the years since its publication, the story has resonated with readers, offering a glimpse into the harrowing experiences of those who lived – and died – in the trenches.

Now, in early June 2024, I find myself once again drawn to the world of *Seven Steps to Eternity*. The soldier's story, his courage, and the brutal realities of war have lingered in my thoughts, calling me back to explore further. It is a strange but compelling feeling to return to a narrative that has already been given life – to add new dimensions and perspectives that time and reflection have brought to the surface.

The first book was a poignant exploration of sacrifice and loss, centred on a young man who faced the ultimate test of character on the battlefield. With this book we connect once again with Jim, and find out what he has been up to in the intervening years. He was only eighteen years old when he was caught in the chaos and carnage of the Somme, a moment that defined his existence and marked the end of his earthly journey. Through his eyes, we witnessed the tragedy of war and the fleeting nature of life – themes that remain as powerful today as they were a century ago.

As I sit down to pen this follow-up, I am reminded of the soldier's bravery and the lessons his story imparts. The intervening years have provided me with new insights and a deeper understanding of the human spirit's resilience in the face of unimaginable adversity. This book is not merely a continuation but an expansion, delving into the enduring impact of his life and death on those he left behind and on the broader tapestry of history.

Writing again about a character who has become so intimately connected to my own creative journey is both a challenge and a privilege. The passage of time has allowed me to view his story through a different lens – one that is shaped by a world that has itself seen profound changes. It is my hope that this new instalment will honour the memory of that young soldier and the countless others who shared his fate, whilst offering readers a fresh perspective on their continuing legacy.

Seven Steps to Eternity was a story of the past, yet its themes are timeless. As we move forward into the sequel, I invite you to join me once again on this journey – one that bridges the gap between history and the present, between the fallen and the living. Together, let us explore what it means to be human, to endure, and to find hope in the shadows of despair.

Stephen Turoff

1

It Begins

It was a late Friday evening when my partner and I, utterly exhausted from a long day of decorating the lounge, finally decided to call it a night. The house was quiet, bathed in the soft glow of the bedside lamp as we climbed into bed. After a murmured goodnight, I quickly slipped into the embrace of sleep.

A few hours must have passed when I felt a tug at the duvet. In my half-awake state, I dismissed it as my partner's restless movements and pulled the cover back over me. It happened again, this time with more insistence. Half-asleep, I mumbled to my partner, 'Stop pulling the duvet off me'. Her drowsy reply came, 'It's not me'.

Startled, I tightened my grip on the duvet and tried to return to the refuge of sleep. But peace was short-lived. The third time, the duvet was yanked from my grasp with such force that it startled me fully awake. An unmistakable, eerie laugh echoed through the room – a laugh I hadn't heard in decades but recognized instantly. My heart pounded in my chest as the room's air grew heavy with a presence both familiar and otherworldly.

'Jim, what do you want at this hour?', I demanded, my voice a mix of frustration and anxiety. Jim was my old writing partner from 30 years ago – except he had passed on. We had spent many months together, crafting his life story and recounting his tragic death at the Battle of the Somme. Our book, *Seven Steps to Eternity*, had been a profound success, chronicling his journey from the battlefield to the afterlife. It had taken everything out of me, pouring my soul into that tale, and I had vowed never to pen another.

Yet here he was, lingering in the spectral twilight between sleep and waking, insisting I return to the quill. His presence filled the room, a tangible force that brought back memories of our long nights of writing and his ethereal guidance. The spectral chill hung in the air as his laughter faded, replaced by a sense of purpose and urgency that seemed to seep into my bones.

In the silent, haunting hours of the night, it became clear that Jim was not ready to let go. The afterlife still had tales to tell, and he wanted me, once again, to be their scribe.

That night, as the shadows grew long and the moon cast its silvery glow across my study, a sense of resolve crystallized within me. Jim's spectral presence loomed, his words echoing through my mind with an urgency that transcended the realm of the living. I felt his silent plea, a haunting insistence that I bring his story to life.

With a deep breath, I made a solemn vow, a commitment to Jim and to the restless spirit of his unfinished tale. I would sit at my computer each day, devoting time to capturing his words, weaving his thoughts into the fabric of my own. Yet there was a condition to this pact that I needed my rest. No more nocturnal visitations that drained the colour from my dreams and left me in a twilight of fatigue. Jim, sensing the weight of my need, gave a silent nod, an ethereal agreement that he would respect my slumber. We had struck a deal: I would write his story, and he would let me sleep.

*

It was 5 am. The dawn broke gently, casting a warm, golden light through the curtains. My partner stirred beside me, her presence a comforting anchor in the reality of a new day. As she sipped her morning coffee, the events of the night tumbled from my lips. Jim visited again, I began, my voice a whisper over the steaming brew. We've come to an understanding. I'll write his words each day, but he must leave me to my sleep.

She arched an eyebrow, a faint smile playing on her lips. Her eyes, sharp and unwavering, held not a hint of disbelief. She was a woman grounded in the here and now, her philosophy rooted in the practical and the tangible.

'Well', she said, her tone brisk and unwavering, 'you better get on with it'.

There was no room for hesitation in her words. Her no-nonsense attitude left no space for the procrastination of tomorrow. She believed firmly in the power of the present, in seizing each moment with purpose and determination.

As she turned back to her coffee, I felt a surge of determination course through me. The day awaited, and with it, the task of giving voice to Jim's unfinished tale. The keyboard beckoned, a silent witness to the promise I had made in the ghostly hours of the night. And so, with a heart steeled by my partner's resolute encouragement and a mind buzzing with the echoes of the spectral, I sat down to write, ready to fulfil the pact that bound me to Jim and his haunting story.

As the hours of the morning deepened, my thoughts turned to Jim. The stillness of the house seemed to amplify my anticipation, each tick of the clock echoing like a heartbeat. 'I'm ready, Jim. Where are you?' I whispered into the silence, my voice barely more than a breath, hoping to summon the spectre who had become my otherworldly muse.

I sat in my chair, eyes darting across the shadows that danced on the walls, waiting for the tell-tale chill or the faint whisper that signalled his presence. Minutes stretched into what felt like an eternity. The anticipation gnawed at me, a creeping unease that began to feel almost oppressive. Restless, I stood and made my way to the kitchen, the hum of the refrigerator and the soft clinking of the kettle offering a comforting counterpoint to the eerie quiet. The ritual of making tea was a small act of defiance against the ghostly tension that had settled over me.

As the hot liquid swirled in my cup, its steam curling upward like a ghost of its own, I returned to my chair, hoping the warmth would settle my nerves. I took a sip, letting the heat seep into me, and leaned back, my body slowly easing into the familiar contours of the seat.

Suddenly, a cold, forceful hand struck my back, and a voice – sharp and startling – pierced the quiet. 'Here I am!' The words slammed into me like a thunderclap, jolting my senses into high alert. My grip on the cup faltered, and hot tea splashed over the rim, spilling down my arm and narrowly missing my computer.

'Jim!', I gasped, the shock turning into a growl of frustration. The ghostly slap had sent a jolt through my body, scattering my thoughts and nearly ruining my equipment. I bit back a string of curses, my pulse pounding in my ears. For a moment, I was paralyzed by the absurdity of the situation – a ghost appearing with the tact of a jackhammer, and me, sitting there drenched in tea.

I turned, my eyes wide with a mix of irritation and disbelief, only to see the air shimmer where Jim's presence had manifested. His spectral form flickered, as if amused by my dishevelled state. He hovered there, insubstantial yet palpably real, a ghostly smirk playing on his lips. I muttered something dark, shaking tea from my hands and glaring at the phantom who had once again disrupted my peace.

Jim's laugh was a low, haunting echo, reverberating through the room like the sound of distant thunder. 'Ready to write now?', he teased, his eyes glinting with a mischief that seemed out of place for a spirit seeking to have his story told.

I took a deep breath, trying to steady the racing of my heart. 'Yes, Jim. Ready as I'll ever be', I replied, my voice steadier than I felt. With a resigned sigh, I set my cup down, wiped the remnants of tea from my arm, and turned to the computer. The early morning was far from over, and the story awaited, demanding to be told. The ghost had made his presence known in no uncertain terms, and I had a promise to keep.

The room seemed to grow colder as Jim's spectral form solidified before me, the edges of his presence shimmering like a heat mirage on a scorching day. His eyes, though ghostly and insubstantial, bore into mine with an intensity that spoke of untold stories and unfulfilled legacies.

'Let's get started', he said, his voice a chilling whisper that seemed to resonate from another realm. The words hung in the air, heavy with the weight of untold history. There was a pause, a pregnant silence where the world seemed to hold its breath, waiting for the tales he was about to unearth.

As Jim began to speak, the room around us seemed to fade, the ordinary confines of my study dissolving into the ether. His voice, though soft, carried the power of ages past, painting vivid pictures of his existence in the spirit world. He spoke of the days following the First and Second World Wars, a time when the world above and the world below were in tumultuous flux.

'After the First War ended', Jim began, his tone imbued with a mix of solemnity and reverence, 'the spirit world was awash with the echoes of countless souls. Soldiers, civilians, innocents – they all arrived in waves, their lives snuffed out in the throes of conflict. The realm was a sea of confusion and despair.'

As he recounted these events, I could almost see the scenes he described – ethereal beings drifting through a fog of uncertainty, searching for purpose and peace. Jim's voice grew stronger, his spectral form flickering with the intensity of his memories.

'There were councils', he continued, 'gatherings of spirits who sought to guide the newly arrived souls. We tried to help them find solace, to make sense of the sudden end of their earthly existence. I became a part of these efforts, learning to navigate the vast expanse of the spirit world, to offer comfort and understanding where I could.'

His words conjured images of spectral assemblies, ghostly figures huddled together in solemn discourse, their forms illuminated by the soft glow of their lingering life force. The air around us seemed to shimmer with the energy of these unseen gatherings. Each word Jim spoke pulled me deeper into his world.

'Then came the Second World War.' Jim's voice darkened, taking on a tone of sorrow and determination. 'The devastation was unimaginable. The influx of souls was even greater, their anguish and torment more profound. The spirit world struggled under the weight of so much loss, so much unfulfilled potential.'

He paused, his gaze distant, as if recalling the overwhelming tide of sorrow that swept through the afterlife. I could almost feel the chill of his memories, the despair that clung to each newly arrived soul. Jim's spectral form wavered, his translucent figure flickering like a candle in a draft.

'We were tested', he said, his voice barely more than a whisper now. 'Those of us who had taken on the role of guides were pushed to our limits. We had to find new ways to help, new methods to soothe the countless spirits who arrived, shattered and broken by the horrors they had endured.'

The weight of his words pressed down on me, the gravity of the spirit world's struggle resonating through the quiet of my study. It was a harrowing tale, one that spoke of unseen battles and the relentless effort to bring peace to those caught in the wake of war.

'But it wasn't all despair.' Jim's voice softened, a glimmer of hope threading through the darkness. 'There were moments of light, of triumph. We discovered that even in the afterlife, there is room for healing and growth. Some spirits found peace, found ways to move beyond their earthly suffering. We learned that the bonds of love and friendship could endure beyond death, offering a beacon of hope in the most profound darkness.'

His words hung in the air, a testament to the resilience of the human spirit, even beyond the veil of mortality. Jim's gaze met mine, and in that moment I felt a profound connection to the countless souls whose stories he carried.

As his tale came to a close, the room seemed to breathe again, the ordinary sounds of the day seeping back into my consciousness. I was left in awe of the unseen struggles and triumphs of the spirit world, a realm as complex and vivid as our own.

'Thank you, Jim', I whispered, my voice barely audible, 'for sharing this with me'.

He gave a slow nod, his form flickering with a spectral light. 'There is more to tell', he said softly. 'But for now, let's rest. We'll continue tomorrow.'

With that, his presence began to fade, the room growing warmer as the chill of the spectral world receded. I sat back in my chair, the enormity of what I had just heard settling over me like a heavy cloak. There was much work ahead, a story to be told that transcended the boundaries of life and death. And I was the chosen vessel to bring it to life.

As I closed my eyes, the faintest smile crossed my lips. For the first time in a week, I knew I would sleep soundly, my dreams untroubled by ghostly visitations. Tomorrow, the journey would continue.

2

Karma, Cause and Effect

'How did you get on with the book yesterday?' my partner asked, her voice filled with curiosity and concern.

I looked up from my reverie, her question pulling me back into the present. 'I never really realized what a dramatic effect Jim's story would have on me', I replied, my tone betraying the swirl of emotions that had gripped me. The memory of Jim's haunting words and his ethereal presence still lingered, like a ghost at the edge of my consciousness. I felt the weight of his story pressing on my soul, each chapter a heavy stone adding to the burden.

She gave me a reassuring smile, a gesture meant to lift my spirits. 'Well, you wrote his first book. I'm sure you will be able to write this one too', she said, her confidence in me unwavering.

Her faith was a lifeline, and I clung to it as I made my way downstairs, the wooden steps creaking under the weight of my thoughts. The kitchen was bathed in the soft light of dawn, the calm before the storm of creativity that I hoped would soon strike. As I poured myself a cup of tea, the steam rising in delicate spirals, I felt a sense of anticipation. The warmth of the cup in my hands was a small comfort against the chill of uncertainty that had settled in my bones.

With my tea in hand, I moved to my study, the familiar hum of the computer a constant in my otherwise turbulent world. I settled into my chair, the leather creaking softly as I leaned back, and stared at the blank screen in front of me.

'Come on, Jim', I whispered, my voice barely more than a breath. 'I'm ready.'

I closed my eyes and waited, hoping to feel that unmistakable tug from the other side, the signal that Jim was ready to share more of his story. The air seemed to thicken, and I could almost sense his presence, a faint shimmer at the edge of my awareness. My fingers hovered over the keyboard, ready to capture every word, every nuance of his tale.

Minutes passed, the silence around me deepening, and I began to wonder if today would be the day he would remain silent. But just as doubt began to creep in, I felt a sudden jolt, as if a spark of electricity had shot through me. My eyes flew open, and there it was – a new chapter, unfolding in my mind, vivid and urgent.

Jim's voice, distant yet clear, began to fill the room, weaving a tapestry of words that I hurried to transcribe. The story poured out of him, raw and unfiltered, and I was merely the conduit, the scribe tasked with bringing his tale to life.

As I typed, the words flowed effortlessly, the barrier between our worlds blurring until it felt as though Jim was right there beside me, guiding my hands across the keyboard. His story was one of redemption and loss, of love and betrayal, and it resonated with a depth that I had not anticipated.

'After I died', Jim began, his voice resonating with a quiet intensity that sent shivers down my spine, 'my parents were overwhelmed by guilt, a crushing weight that bore down on them day and night.'

The air in the room grew colder, and I could almost feel the oppressive atmosphere of despair that must have enveloped his family. Jim's presence was palpable, a spectral entity hovering in the space between us, and his words painted a vivid picture of his parents' anguish. Their faces, etched with sorrow, flickered before my eyes like a ghostly slideshow.

Jim's voice trembled slightly, laden with the sorrow and confusion of his untimely end. 'I wanted so desperately to let them know I was still alive, even though my body lay dead in the mud. My life snuffed out by a piece of shrapnel that tore through my chest.' His words echoed with a haunting clarity, conjuring images of that fateful moment on the battlefield. 'I remember the searing pain, the hot, sticky blood soaking into the cold earth beneath me', he continued, his tone raw with emotion. 'Everything around me was chaos – the screams of the wounded, the relentless pounding of artillery. But amidst the cacophony, there was a strange, eerie silence inside me as I felt life slipping away.'

His voice grew softer, tinged with a lingering incomprehension. 'It was the most bewildering and terrifying time of my life. One moment, I was fighting, clinging to every shred of life. The next, I was hovering above my own body, looking down at the lifeless shell that had once been me.' Jim paused, and I could almost see him reliving that moment, the horror and the confusion of it all. 'I could see my parents' faces in my mind, their expressions twisted with grief and regret. They were hundreds of miles away, yet I could feel their pain as if it were my own.'

Jim took a deep, shuddering breath, and I felt a surge of empathy for the struggle he had faced.

'I tried to reach out to them', Jim continued, 'to let them know that I wasn't truly gone, that my spirit still lingered. But I was trapped, caught between worlds, unable to bridge the gap. I was a silent observer to their suffering, powerless to ease their pain.'

Tears welled up in my eyes as I listened to his heart-wrenching tale. Jim's words cut through me, laying bare the agony of a soul yearning for connection, for a chance to reassure the ones he loved that death had not taken him entirely.

Jim cried out: 'I wanted to scream, to tell them that I was still here', he whispered, his voice barely more than a breath. 'But all I could do was watch, helpless, as they drowned in their sorrow.'

Jim's story hung heavy in the air, a poignant reminder of the invisible threads that bind us to those we love, even beyond death. As I sat there, my fingers trembling on the keyboard, I knew that his tale was more than just a recounting of past events – it was a testament to the enduring power of love, and the haunting echoes of a life cut tragically short.

The room fell silent, the weight of his words settling over me like a shroud. Jim's presence seemed to recede, his story now told, but the impact of his message remained. I stared at the screen, the words shimmering in the dim light, and I felt a profound sense of responsibility. Jim's voice, though silent now, had left an indelible mark on my soul.

'Do you need a rest?' I asked Jim, my voice trembling with concern as the weight of his fatigue seemed to grow heavier with each step.

He paused for a moment, the shadows of his past etched deeply in the lines of his face. His eyes, once bright and full of life, now held a sombre wisdom. 'No', he replied, his voice a soft but resolute whisper, almost as if the admission carried a profound gravity. 'I have long got over those feelings. I had to', he continued, each word tinged with a mix of sorrow and steely determination.

He glanced up at the dim, flickering light that barely pierced the oppressive gloom surrounding us, as if searching for something unseen. 'They were holding me back', he confessed, his tone growing more intense, laden with the echoes of countless battles fought within his soul. 'They kept me a prisoner of the lower astral plane', he added, his voice cracking slightly under the weight of the memories that surfaced – a place of torment and despair, where the lost and the broken wander endlessly.

Jim's eyes flickered with a haunted intensity, the depth of his struggle laid bare before me. 'Every step away from that darkness was a battle', he said, his gaze locking onto mine with a fierce resolve. 'A battle I could not afford to lose. Because losing meant losing myself, forever.'

His words hung in the air between us, heavy and fraught with unspoken pain. I could almost feel the invisible chains that once bound him, the relentless grip of the lower astral plane that sought to drag him back into its shadowy depths. But there he stood, defiant, no longer a prisoner but a warrior, forged in the fires of his own suffering.

'That day, I was one of the lucky few, narrowly escaping the calamity that claimed countless lives', Jim stated, 'as I stumbled through the dense, disorienting fog, lost and bewildered, a figure materialized beside me. He introduced himself as "the Bear", a name that suited him perfectly at first glance. His massive frame and commanding presence loomed like a steadfast guardian in the midst of the swirling, relentless mist. "But my family calls me Bill", he added, his voice a low rumble that matched his formidable stature. Together, we stumbled through this eerie purgatory, the acrid taste of smoke and fear thick in the air. The mist, dense and unyielding, clung to us like the remnants of war itself, obscuring the ground beneath our feet and the sky above our heads. We were adrift in a void where time and space seemed to collapse, the screams and echoes of battle still reverberating in our ears.

'In that suffocating gloom, we suddenly encountered a group of beings who moved with a grace and purpose that contrasted starkly with the devastation around them. They were the Rescuers, radiant figures whose very presence exuded warmth and light, cutting through the despair that had enveloped us. I felt an overwhelming surge of gratitude and relief as they approached, their eyes reflecting a kindness that seemed almost otherworldly.

'"Thank God", I whispered, my voice trembling with the weight of survival. These were not just ordinary souls; they were our saviours, tasked with the solemn duty of gathering the newly fallen and guiding us to a sanctuary beyond the reach of war's cruel grasp. Their mission was to rescue us from the abyss of suffering, to lift us from the battlefield strewn with shattered lives and carry us to a realm of peace and solace. Yet, not all who roamed this astral battleground were benevolent. We were warned of other entities, dark and malevolent, who prowled the fog with a sinister intent. These predators of the soul sought out the newly slain, preying upon our raw, exposed emotions. Their goal was to ensnare us in the web of our own despair, to feed on our fear and hopelessness until we were dragged down into the depths of hell itself.

'As the Bear and I followed the Rescuers, the threat of these shadowy figures loomed large in our minds. We could feel their presence lurking at the edges of the mist, waiting for a moment of weakness to strike. Every step we took was a desperate struggle to stay in the light, to hold on to the hope that these good souls offered, and to avoid the darkness that threatened to consume us entirely. In the end, it was the unwavering resolve of the Rescuers and the unexpected bond I formed with the Bear that saved me. They led us through the mist, away from the battlefield of carnage and toward a sanctuary where the echoes of war could no longer reach us. And as we stepped into the light, leaving the fog and the horrors behind, I knew we had escaped not just the grip of death, but the clutches of a fate far more terrifying.

'Stephen, would you believe we were among a hundred and fifty other souls claimed by destiny on that fateful day, our lives abruptly severed from the world we knew. Guided through the veil of death, we were ushered into a vast, ethereal hall. The air was thick with an otherworldly aura, the walls shimmering with an unsettling, spectral light. The crowd around me – men, women, children – stood silent, their faces etched with the haunting realization of their demise.

'At the front of this ghostly assembly, upon a raised platform, stood a figure of authority – Captain Marsh. His presence commanded attention, a sentinel in a military uniform that seemed to flicker between the tangible and the ethereal. His eyes, deep and unyielding, scanned the crowd as he began to speak.

'"Welcome", he said, his voice reverberating through the hall, carrying a weight that felt both comforting and inescapable. "You are no longer of the living. You have crossed into a realm between worlds, a place of reckoning and reflection. I am Captain Marsh, and I am here to guide you through the next steps of your journey."'

Jim continued speaking: 'As Captain Marsh words settled over us like a shroud, a murmur of recognition rippled through the gathered souls. We were in the presence of a guardian of the dead, a shepherd for those who had lost their way in the cataclysmic chaos of the day. The rest, as you know from our first book, is a tale of discovery and redemption, a chronicle of the paths we walked in that shadowy realm, guided by the enigmatic Captain Marsh.

'In the labyrinthine corridors of time, the present moment stands as an extraordinary confluence of forces, where the echoes of the past intertwine with the burgeoning whispers of the future. The present moment is a unique blend of the past's legacy and the future's promise. Your world stands at a crossroads, where technological advancement, societal change, and environmental challenges converge, shaping the fabric of your daily life.

'In the realm of Earth technology, you have witnessed an unprecedented acceleration. Artificial intelligence (AI) and machine learning have moved from being niche technologies to mainstream applications, influencing nearly every industry. Societal norms and structures are also evolving rapidly. The pandemic years have left an indelible mark on social behaviour and work environments.

'The present time reflects a collective consciousness grappling with complex issues, striving towards inclusivity, and demanding accountability and action from institutions and leaders. The climate crisis is one of the most pressing issues of your time, Stephen. The present moment is marked by an urgent need for action to combat global warming and environmental degradation. The increasing frequency of extreme weather events, rising sea levels and biodiversity loss underscore the necessity for sustainable practices and policies. The present is a moment of significant transformation, driven by a complex web of influences and marked by the enduring human spirit. It is a time that demands awareness, adaptability, and collective effort to shape a future that is equitable, sustainable, and hopeful to all.'

'Good God, Jim, did you eat a dictionary?', I blurted out, barely containing my shock. The sheer sophistication of his language was almost laughable. 'In just 30 years, you've transformed from a regular guy to someone who sounds like they're auditioning for a role in a Shakespearean play. Are you sure you're not hiding a thesaurus somewhere? I mean, what happened to the guy who used to yell at me if I was not at the computer on time? Now you're tossing around phrases like "labyrinthine corridors of time", as if you're delivering a grand lecture at a forum! It's as if you've suddenly transformed into a sage, standing at the helm of a cosmic symposium, unravelling the intricate and boundless tapestry of existence with the eloquence and fervour of a seasoned orator. You're not just speaking; you're weaving an epic narrative that dances across the eons, traversing the winding, enigmatic passageways of history and destiny – ha ha ha! It's as if, in this very moment, you and I have been possessed by the spirit of the universe itself, and you to channelling the wisdom of the ages into a single, electrifying discourse that leaves us all in awe of the vast, uncharted expanses of time.'

A hearty, resonant laughter erupted from deep within Jim, filling the room with an unexpected vibrancy. His eyes sparkled with a mix of amusement and revelation, a smile tugging at the corners of his mouth. 'You know', he began, his voice carrying a warmth that was almost tangible, 'I was made to study over there. At first, I thought it was just another challenge thrown my way, another hurdle in the relentless race of life. But Chan, my spirit guide, made me go.'

He paused, glancing out of the window at the garden bathed in the golden hues of the midday sun. 'I remember the distant sounds of students' chatter and the occasional rustling of leaves as I walked to the lecture hall. We have many halls of learning there', he continued, turning his gaze back with a newfound clarity. 'I'm glad I did. Truly. This place, this experience – it's given me a better insight into your world and, in ways I hadn't anticipated, into my own.'

Jim's eyes took on a faraway look, as if he were peering into the depths of his past and the possibilities of his future. 'Over there, I've discovered layers to myself I never knew existed. I've learned to see the world through different lenses, to appreciate the vast tapestry of cultures, ideas and dreams that weave our lives together. It's like I've been handed the keys to a treasure chest brimming with perspectives and wisdom.'

He leaned forward, his expression earnest now. 'And in understanding your world better, I've come to understand mine too.

The things I took for granted, the beliefs I held without question – they've all been challenged and reshaped. It's as if this journey was meant to peel back the layers, to reveal a deeper truth about who I am and where I come from.'

Jim's voice softened, but the intensity in his eyes remained. 'So yes, I was made to study there, but it's been more than just an education. It's been an awakening. And for that, I am profoundly grateful.

'Knowledge, in all its splendour, is a beacon illuminating the vast expanse of human potential.' Jim continued. 'It is a magnificent force, capable of unravelling the mysteries of the universe and propelling civilization to astonishing heights. Yet knowledge alone is a double-edged sword – brilliant in its promise, perilous in its absence of guidance. Without the steadying hand of wisdom, knowledge becomes a mere instrument of ignorance, a Pandora's box unleashed upon the world. Wisdom is the compass that navigates the uncharted seas of knowledge, tempering its power with insight and understanding. It is the quiet voice urging caution in the face of innovation, the discerning eye that perceives the long shadows cast by short-term gains.

'Look around you, witness the marvels that knowledge has bestowed upon you – the technological wonders, the vast repositories of information at your fingertips, the incredible feats of science and engineering. You soar higher than ever before, touching the stars and unravelling the fabric of reality itself. Yet in the same breath, observe the scars of heedless ambition. The environmental degradation, the ethical dilemmas of unchecked advancements, the social fractures driven by the relentless pursuit of progress. Consider the grandeur of your achievements and the haunting consequences of their misapplication. Knowledge, untethered by wisdom, has become a force of both creation and destruction. The same intellect that harnesses the atom for energy also wields it for annihilation. The same networks that connect you can divide and manipulate you.

'Wisdom, that profound and elusive companion to knowledge, is the key to a balanced and harmonious world. It is the sage counsel that recognizes when to advance and when to retreat, when to innovate and when to preserve. It is the guardian of our shared humanity, ensuring that our pursuit of knowledge enhances rather than diminishes the human spirit. Reflect upon the world before you. See the brilliance of your collective intellect, and also see the chaos and destruction wrought by knowledge untempered by wisdom. To forge a future that is not only advanced but also *just* and *compassionate*, you must marry our relentless quest for knowledge with the timeless wisdom that guides your actions towards the greater good.'

I asked with bated breath: 'Jim, are you still with Rose?' His response came slowly, laden with an unspoken weight. 'No', he sighed heavily, 'we're still good friends. It's just – she had to move on with her life. In a mystical twist of fate, she was reincarnated amidst the vibrant turmoil of 1970s Denmark, finding herself born into a bustling household already graced with two other children. Destiny wove her a new life, steering her path towards marriage and motherhood, where she now stands as the matriarch of her own loving family.

'Our connection transcends mere mortal bounds. Across the veils of reality, I journey to her side whenever she calls, lending my aid in moments of need. And in those ethereal hours of night, she visits me in her dreams, where we converse deeply, reminiscing about days past and unravelling the mysteries of life itself. These nocturnal dialogues are our sanctuary, where time bends and our spirits intertwine, forging an unbreakable bond that defies the constraints of earthly existence.' There was a fleeting pause, but in that moment I felt a profound sadness emanating from Jim, as if each word he uttered carried the weight of a thousand regrets.

'Jim, could you please explain reincarnation more thoroughly. How does it work? How do past lives influence our current existence?' Could he share the stories of souls moving through different realms, seeking understanding or resolution? I was curious about karma's role in shaping this journey through time.

Jim's voice trembled with the weight of the knowledge he was about to share. 'I can only touch upon this vast ocean of knowledge', he began, his eyes reflecting the depth of what he was about to convey. 'Imagine, if you will, a boundless sea, stretching infinitely in every direction. This sea holds secrets and truths beyond our wildest dreams, depths that no human can fully fathom.'

He paused, letting the gravity of his words sink in. 'And in the midst of this overwhelming expanse, I stand on the shore, a mere speck, able to grasp only a fraction of its immensity. But even this tiny fragment is powerful beyond measure.'

Taking a deep breath, he continued, his voice now a hushed reverence. 'When I sought answers, when the weight of my own questions bore down upon me, I turned to Chan. I asked him the very same questions that now linger in your mind, questions that gnaw at your curiosity and thirst for understanding.'

Jim's gaze became distant, as if he was transported back to that moment. 'Chan looked at me with eyes that seemed to hold the wisdom of ages. And he answered, not with the complexity one might expect, but with a simplicity that held profound truth. His words were like a beacon, cutting through the fog of uncertainty.'

Drawing himself back to the present, Jim met my eyes with a steady resolve. 'And now', he said, 'I will share with you the very answer Chan gave to me. A simple answer that, like a single drop of water, holds the essence of that vast ocean, ready to ripple through your consciousness and awaken the depths of your own understanding.

'Stephen, Karma is a foundational concept in the spiritual philosophies of Hinduism, Buddhism, and Jainism, and is often perceived as the universal law of cause and effect. It is a mystical principle that transcends simple moral binaries, delving into the deeper mechanics of the cosmos and the soul's journey through time. Karma embodies the idea that every action, thought and intention sends ripples through the fabric of the universe, ultimately returning to the originator in some form or another. This principle underlines the interconnectedness of all beings and the profound unity of existence.

'In its mystical essence, karma is not a punitive system of rewards and punishments but rather a cosmic law of balance and spiritual growth. It operates on the principle that every action generates energy that influences future circumstances. These energies, whether positive or negative, are like seeds sown into the universe. They sprout and manifest as life experiences that reflect the nature of their origin. Positive actions, rooted in compassion and kindness, typically result in favourable outcomes, while negative actions, born of ignorance or malice, often lead to suffering and hardship. This process, however, is not meant to be seen as retribution but as opportunities for the soul to learn and evolve.

'The mystical aspect of karma is further deepened by its operation across multiple lifetimes. According to spiritual traditions, the soul is eternal and experiences a series of births and deaths, each life a new chapter in an ongoing journey of spiritual evolution. Karma, in this context, acts as the recorder of the soul's actions, preserving the consequences of each thought, word and deed. These accumulated karmas, known as *samskaras* or imprints, shape the circumstances of future births, influencing not only one's character and predispositions but also the experiences one encounters.

'This cyclical nature of karma and rebirth, known as *samsara*, underscores the concept of karma as a continuous feedback loop. The challenges and joys experienced in one life are often the result of actions from previous ones. This understanding instils a deep sense of responsibility, as every action taken in the present can have long-lasting effects on one's future. It encourages individuals to cultivate virtues such as patience, compassion and mindfulness, knowing that these qualities generate positive karma that can lead to spiritual liberation, or *moksha*.

'The elusive and often hidden workings of karma invite a journey into self-awareness and introspection. Since the consequences of our actions are not always immediately apparent, karma encourages us to look beyond the surface and understand the deeper implications of our behaviour. It teaches the importance of intention; even actions that seem outwardly good can generate negative karma if driven by selfish motives. This subtlety makes karma a complex and profound spiritual doctrine, pushing individuals to align their actions with their highest values and intentions.

'Karma is intricately linked with the concept of *dharma*, or righteous duty. Dharma represents the moral and ethical obligations that one must follow according to their nature, role and position in life. It is believed that by fulfilling one's dharma, a person aligns themselves with the cosmic order and thus generates positive karma. This alignment is not just a path to personal peace but a contribution to the harmony of the universe as a whole. Each person's dharma is unique, reflecting their individual talents, circumstances and spiritual path. By discovering and living in accordance with one's dharma, a person not only fulfils their purpose but also helps to balance the cosmic scales. Are you getting all this, Stephen?', Jim asked rather sharply.

'Yes – yes I am, just concentrating, that's all!', I replied.

'OK, then I'll continue. The mystical journey of karma ultimately leads to the realization of the interconnectedness of all life. It fosters a deep awareness that all beings are interwoven into the same cosmic tapestry, where every action affects the whole. This awareness encourages a life of compassion, empathy and selflessness. Understanding karma means recognizing that harm done to another is harm done to oneself, just as acts of kindness uplift the entire fabric of existence.

'Karma is far more than a mechanism of cosmic justice; it is a profound spiritual teacher guiding souls towards enlightenment. It reveals the deeper workings of the universe, showing that every moment is an opportunity for growth and self-realization. Through understanding and aligning with the principles of karma, individuals can transcend the cycle of *samsara*, achieving ultimate liberation and unity with the divine. This mystical journey emphasizes the sacred interconnectedness of all beings, urging us to live with integrity, compassion and wisdom.'

Jim laughed suddenly as he finished his story. 'Well, that's what Chan told me. All I know is, when it's time to reincarnate, you supposedly go to a special hall. There, your karmas are then displayed to you, and with those you love standing by your side. They encourage you to let go. You then go into a meditation and you drift off to a sleeplike state, only to awaken as a child in another country, born into a family that best suits your karmic debts and destiny.

'People say it's like a dream – you wake up with fragmented memories of your past life, if any at all. Some believe you carry lessons from your previous life, but it's all a mystery, isn't it?' Jim chuckled, clearly amused by the fantastical nature of the tale he was sharing.

Hours later, I leaned back, exhausted but exhilarated. The screen was filled with Jim's words, a testament to the connection that transcended the boundary between life and death. I knew then that this book would be more than just a story – it would be a legacy, a bridge between our worlds.

I took a deep breath, feeling the last remnants of Jim's presence fade away, and allowed myself a small, triumphant smile. The journey was far from over, but for the first time, I felt truly ready to take it.

Dinner was an extraordinary experience. As soon as I sat down and took that first bite, it hit me just how ravenous I had been without even realizing it. The rich aroma and flavours awakened a hunger deep within me, one I hadn't fully acknowledged until that moment. The food was a symphony of tastes and textures, each bite more satisfying than the last.

As I relished the meal, my partner's voice brought me back to the present, asking about the day's writing. It was a simple question, yet it felt like an invitation to delve into the creative journey I had embarked on earlier. The warmth of the meal, combined with the comfort of our conversation, created a perfect ending to the day.

3

Meeting my Spiritual Guide

'You mentioned Chan, your spiritual guide, who drew you towards the Hall of Learning. Please, reveal the essence of this encounter. How did his ethereal presence lead you towards enlightenment? Describe for us the vivid impact of his influence and the profound resonance of his teachings within those sacred walls. What mysteries did he unfold for you? What challenges did he place on your path? Share with us, in the quiet echoes of whispered truths, the transformative power that Chan brought to your journey.'

'Wow, Stephen. That's some demand! I'll do my best. Well, Chan is an enigma. I'll tell you how it started.' Jim reflected back to the time of his induction to the world of knowledge. 'The call of Chan, the ethereal guide who illuminates my path to wisdom, is a tale woven in the delicate threads of both seen and unseen realms. Imagine, if you will, a presence not of corporeal form but of a deeper essence, whispering through the veils of consciousness, drawing one into the sanctum of enlightenment with an irresistible allure. It began on a serene day in spirit. On that occasion I was with Rose, the air tinged with a mystic quietude, and the spirit world seemed to dissolve into shadows. In that stillness, Chan's presence emerged, not as a figure of flesh and bone, but as a gentle, resonant vibration that hummed within my very soul. His voice, a melody of the cosmos, spoke in a language that bypassed the ear and resonated directly with the heart, compelling me to rise and seek the Hall of Learning. Rose was most understanding as I had to leave rather suddenly.

'Guided by this unseen hand, I found myself before the Hall of Learning, a grand edifice of light and shadow, its architecture shifting and shimmering with each breath I took. The doors, immense and adorned with symbols that pulsed with ancient wisdom, opened silently at my approach. Inside, the air was thick with the scent of aged parchment and the faint, lingering echoes of countless seekers who had come before me.

'As I stepped within, Chan's essence enveloped me, merging with the air I breathed, the ground I walked upon. He did not teach through words alone, but through a profound communion of thoughts and feelings, an exchange that transcended mere dialogue. In the Hall, there were no teachers or students, only souls in varying stages of awakening, guided by the same light that Chan imparted.

'He unveiled mysteries not through exposition but through experiences. In one moment, I stood at the edge of a vast chasm, peering into the void of my own ignorance. Chan's guidance was the bridge that spanned this chasm, each step I took revealing more about my inner self and the cosmos beyond.

'The path Chan laid before me was not one of ease. It was fraught with trials that tested my resolve and expanded my perception. One such trial was the Mirror of Reflection, where I was compelled to confront my deepest fears and desires, to see them not as enemies but as facets of my own being. In another, the Labyrinth of Silence, I wandered through corridors of stillness, where only by quieting the noise within could I find my way.

'Each trial was a lesson in disguise, a challenge to transcend the limits of my understanding and embrace a more profound truth. Chan's presence was a constant, a beacon that illuminated the path even when the way seemed lost in darkness.

'Through these encounters, the transformative power of Chan became evident. His influence was not to change the external world, but to transform the inner landscape. Under his guidance, I learned to navigate the intricacies of my own mind and spirit, to find balance amidst chaos, and to see the interconnectedness of all things. Chan did not simply impart knowledge; he awakened a deeper wisdom within me, a resonance that continues to guide me through life's myriad journeys. His teachings are a living force, a perpetual dance of light and shadow that shapes my understanding and enriches my existence.

'To speak of Chan is to delve into a realm where the sacred and the mundane merge, where every step is both a question and an answer, where every breath is a whisper of the eternal. His presence, though intangible, is as real as the ground beneath my feet, and his guidance as clear as the stars that chart the night sky. Through Chan, I have come to see that the Hall of Learning is not a distant place, but a state of being, always within reach, always inviting us to enter and discover the boundless mysteries of our own souls.

'When I first arrived in this world, the Chan I encountered was vastly different from the one I know now. Back then, he was more like a guide for beginners, a beacon for the uninitiated. My initial days were filled with uncertainty and the steep learning curves of mastering the basics. Chan was patient and steadfast, helping me navigate through the foundational elements that I needed to grasp. In those early days, my focus was on figuring out the basics – understanding the culture, learning how to communicate by telepathy, and just getting by. It was a period of adjustment, and Chan provided the support and structure I needed. He wasn't just a mentor; he was a constant presence, adapting his guidance to my evolving needs. Whether it was the simplest tasks or the more complex nuances of this new realm, Chan was there, steady and reliable.

'As the years went by and I became more accustomed to my surroundings, the nature of our relationship began to change. Chan evolved with me. He was no longer just a mentor who helped me with the basics; he became an advisor and an encourager. It was during this time that he started to push me towards broader horizons. He recognized potential in me that I hadn't yet seen myself.

'When I began contemplating my future and what kind of work would suit me best, Chan's role became more profound. He was instrumental in guiding me to understand my strengths and passions. He encouraged me to pursue further education, seeing it as a pathway to realizing the truth about myself.

'In every season of my journey, Chan has adapted to my needs. From the early days of learning and adaptation to the later years of ambition and growth, he has been a consistent and evolving force. He's truly a being for all seasons, a mentor whose presence and guidance have been invaluable at every stage of my journey here.

'He was not just a mentor; he was my unwavering pillar of strength during the tumultuous battles waged on the lower astral planes. These were not mere skirmishes but ferocious clashes that reverberated through the very fabric of our existence. The lower astral was a realm of shadows and despair, where the echoes of suffering and conflict never ceased. Amidst the chaos, his presence was a beacon, guiding me through the darkest hours of my struggle.

'Harry and Jack, who were mentioned in the first book, have maintained an unbreakable bond with me, a lifeline of communication that was as vital as the air we breathed. We were not alone in our fight; we were warriors in an endless war. Each day brought new confrontations, fresh horrors that demanded our resolve. The battles raged on, relentless and merciless. They churned out souls that were battered and bruised – much like I had been all those years ago.

'These souls, tormented and lost, arrived in our realm, their cries for solace echoing the agony I once knew so intimately. Their distress was a mirror reflecting my own past torment, a haunting reminder of the suffering that once bound me. But with every new soul, I felt a surge of purpose, a fierce determination to stand by them as Chan had stood by me. In the midst of turmoil and chaos, we fought not just for ourselves but for the redemption and peace of countless others, perpetually caught in the relentless storms of the lower astral.'

When I asked Jim if the wars on Earth will ever cease, the answer was stark and sobering:

'Not in your lifetime, nor in countless lifetimes to come', Jim said solemnly, 'for mankind is ensnared, deeply entangled in an unending cycle of power and dominance. The thirst for control courses through human veins like a relentless, poisonous river, staining history with the blood of ambition.

'From the dawn of civilization, empires have risen and crumbled under the weight of their own conquests, each generation inheriting the scars of those before. The cries of the fallen echo through the corridors of time, yet the lessons of their suffering remain unheard. Humanity, blinded by pride and greed, continues to march to the drums of war, unable or unwilling to break free from the shackles of its own making.

'The landscape of Earth is a battlefield etched with the footprints of soldiers, the ruins of cities laid waste by conflict, and the silent, grieving monuments to lives lost. Dreams of peace are fragile whispers in the storm of human strife, fleeting and easily shattered by the harsh reality of human nature. Until humanity can transcend this primitive lust for power to find harmony and compassion within itself, the cycle of war will persist. It is a bleak prophecy, a mirror reflecting your darkest truths. The end of war is not a horizon you will witness, nor your children, nor their descendants, as long as the hearts of men remain consumed by their insatiable hunger for dominion.'

'Jim, would you be willing to recount your latest encounter upon the lower astral plane for us?' My voice trembled slightly, the weight of my question hanging in the charged air.

Jim paused, his gaze distant and haunted. 'Do you truly grasp the immense mental fortitude required to traverse those otherworldly realms, Stephen?', he responded, his voice edged with a mix of weariness and warning.

My eyes widened, a flicker of remembered fear darting across my face. 'I've had my share of encounters with the unknown', I said, a touch of defensiveness in my tone. 'The eerie whispers, the shadows that cling to the edges of consciousness. It's not unfamiliar to me.'

Jim's expression softened, his sternness melting into understanding. 'Forgive me', he murmured, inclining his head slightly. 'I meant no offence. My words were directed more towards enlightening your audience, who might not fully comprehend the perils and the sheer psychic energy demanded by such journeys.'

A heavy silence settled over the room, filled with the echoes of unseen realms and the quiet hum of shared experiences with the supernatural.

'We've barely escaped the turmoil of the astral battlefield', Jim recounted, 'the echoes of our desperate struggle still reverberating in our minds. My comrades and I, weary and battered, are in dire need of respite. This is why I've sought you out, Stephen. Do not mistake my intentions; it's not mere weariness that drives me to you, but a fervent need to unveil the stark, unvarnished reality of war.

'Your readers deserve more than the sanitized versions fed to them by the national press. They must see beyond the glossy headlines and patriotic rhetoric. They must know the truth – the raw, brutal essence of conflict that we endure. The lifeless eyes of fallen friends, the eerie silence that follows a battle's end, and the relentless toll on our souls. It's not just the physical scars we bear but the unseen wounds that bleed within us, haunting our nights and shadowing our days. Only by shedding light on these truths can we hope truly to understand the cost of war. And only through your words, Stephen, can we break through the veil of ignorance that shrouds the grim reality we've lived and fought through.

'The weight of our assignment to the front line in Ukraine pressed down on me like a suffocating shroud. My friends and I had braced ourselves for the worst, but nothing could have prepared us for the sheer devastation that awaited us. It was as if the very soul of the land had been ripped asunder.

'As we approached the heart of the conflict, the air thickened with tension, and the echoes of battle cries and the rumbling of artillery became an oppressive soundtrack to our every step. It was a nightmare come to life, a place where brother fought against brother, friends turned into foes, and enemies clashed with a ferocity born of sheer desperation.

'The landscape was a scarred battlefield, marred by craters from relentless shelling, and the remnants of once-thriving villages now stood as ghostly reminders of what had been lost. The acrid smell of smoke mingled with the scent of fear and despair that hung heavy in the air. In the midst of this chaos, just before we stepped into the abyss, we were called to gather in a makeshift sanctuary, an old, half-destroyed chapel still standing defiantly amidst the ruins. Brother David, our spiritual anchor in this maelstrom, stood at the altar, his eyes reflecting the collective anguish of those around him. With a voice that seemed to carry the weight of the entire war-torn world, he called us to prayer.

'We bowed our heads, seeking solace and strength from the divine, trying to muster some semblance of peace in the face of unimaginable horror. The silence was broken only by the distant sounds of conflict, a stark reminder of what awaited us beyond the fragile walls of the chapel.

'After the prayer, Brother David's words cut through the thick fog of our fear and uncertainty. He spoke with a passion that lit a spark of hope within us, his voice rising and falling like a symphony amidst the cacophony of war. He told us stories of bravery and resilience, of men who had found the courage to rise above the horrors of battle and fight not just for themselves, but for each other. His speech was not just a call to arms but a call to our very souls. He reminded us that amidst the darkness, we are the light, that even in the face of such catastrophic conflict, we could find humanity and compassion. His words wove a tapestry of hope that wrapped around us, giving us the strength to face the inferno that awaited.

'As we prepared to leave the chapel and step into the inferno, the haunting reality of the front line loomed before us. We were about to enter a world where every second could be the last for those who stood upon this battle ground. The ground beneath our feet trembled with the force of explosions. Yes we could feel everything, even though we cannot die, we can still feel fear and pain. But despite the fear gnawing at our hearts, Brother David's voice lingered in our minds, a beacon of hope amidst the darkness. And with that hope, we stepped forward into the chaos, into the disaster that was the front line in Ukraine, ready to face whatever came our way.

'We kept in our units of three: Harry, Jack and myself. The three of us had been together for what felt like an eternity, our bond forged in the furnace of countless battles. We operated like a well-oiled machine, each knowing instinctively what the other would do next, a silent symphony of survival and strategy. The brutal reality of war was that too many young men were torn apart by shrapnel or riddled with bullets, their spirits now wandering the astral plane. Lost and confused, they lingered between worlds, still believing they were alive, ever ready to attack any perceived enemy in their path. In this ghostly aftermath, it became imperative to navigate carefully. Should we encounter Ukrainians or a unit of them, we had to ensure that we blended seamlessly into their ranks. The right uniform, the right dialect – these were the thin lines between us saving them from the lower astrals. It was a lesson we had learned from our last mission, chronicled in the previous volume of our harrowing tales.

'Thanks to my training, I had mastered the art of swift disguise, a skill essential in this theatre of war. Harry and Jack had picked it up as well. Changing clothes instantly wasn't just a trick; it was a necessity, a means of deception and survival. In the chaos of battle, where the enemy could be anyone, anywhere, this ability became one of our greatest assets. It was all done by the power of our thoughts. The change was instant.

'War, we had discovered, demanded more than just courage and resilience. It required adaptability, the ability to become a chameleon, shifting appearances as effortlessly as shadows under the moonlight. In this ruthless landscape, we were more than soldiers. we were quick-change artists, each transformation a crucial manoeuvre.

'In the eerie, mist-shrouded expanse of the astral plane, we stumbled upon an unsettling tableau: a squad of Russian soldiers, locked in a relentless battle with their Ukrainian counterparts. They fought with ferocity, oblivious to the fact that they had died long ago. The realization struck us like a thunderclap – they were trapped in this spectral realm, unaware of their undead condition.

'As we watched, a Ukrainian soldier was struck by a bayonet. He crumpled to the ground, but to our astonishment, within mere moments, he rose again, seemingly untouched by death's finality. It was a grotesque parody of life, a cycle of unending conflict. Here, in the astral plane, the concept of mortality was meaningless, a cruel jest played upon these tormented souls.

'The urgency of our mission surged through us. The dark, malevolent forces of the lower astral realm were converging, drawn to the chaotic energy of the battle. We had to act swiftly to cease the fighting and guide these lost soldiers to peace before the evil entities engulfed them. Jack, ever the quick thinker, proposed a bold strategy.

'"Listen", he said, his voice cutting through the tension, "one of us should disguise as a Russian officer, and the other as a Ukrainian officer. We'll command them to stop fighting, tell them the war is over. It's our only chance to reach them."

'I considered his plan for a moment. It was audacious, but desperation had a way of birthing brilliance. "It just might work, Jack", I agreed, trying to mask the flicker of doubt in my voice with a veneer of calm. Without wasting a second, we thought of ourselves draped in the uniforms of the officers. Jack donned the guise of a Russian officer, his stern demeanour lending credibility to his role, while I assumed the appearance of a Ukrainian commander, hoping to inspire trust, while Harry held back, just in case things went pear-shaped.

'We approached the frenzied soldiers cautiously, our hearts pounding in our chests. As we emerged from the shadows in our new roles, the clamour of battle slowly dwindled to a stunned silence. Eyes wide with disbelief, the soldiers hesitated, their weapons dropping slightly as they processed our sudden appearance.

'"The war is over", Jack shouted, in Russian, his voice commanding and resolute. "Stand down, that's an order!"

'I echoed his sentiment, urging the Ukrainians to cease fire. "Enough! Lay down your arms. We have orders to lead you to safety."

'The effect was instantaneous. The soldiers, disoriented and desperate for relief, began to lower their weapons. Questions erupted from both sides, a torrent of confusion and disbelief, but we quelled them with authoritative gestures. "Follow us", I ordered, trying to maintain an air of unshakeable authority. "There's no time to explain. Just trust us."

'With a mixture of weariness and hope, they obeyed, trailing behind us like lost children. We guided them through the dense fog to a clearing where a circle of our colleagues awaited. These were experts, skilled in the delicate art of awakening souls to the truth of their circumstances. Here, under the protective watch of our allied forces, the soldiers would learn of their fate and find solace. The malevolent forces of the lower astral realms prowled the periphery of our circle, but they dared not cross. We had created a sanctuary, impervious to their dark influence. As the soldiers began to understand the reality of their situation, the weight of centuries-old enmity lifted, replaced by a profound sense of peace.

'In this fragile space between worlds, where time and death had lost their meaning, we had forged a moment of harmony. The soldiers, once enemies in life, now stood united in the shared experience of their spectral existence. And as we watched them begin their journey to rest, we knew that, for now, the evil lurking in the shadows had been held at bay.

'A message came like a lightning bolt to my mind, a sudden and urgent transmission from Brother David. His mental voice crackled with an intensity that demanded immediate attention. "Go at once to the new coordinates", he implored. "The lower astrals have breached our defences." His words were laced with a gravity that sent shivers down my spine. This wasn't just a call to action; it was a desperate plea for help. Instantly, the message reverberated in the minds of the other two, each one of us absorbing the dire situation unfolding. The lower astrals breaking through our lines signified a catastrophe; they were malevolent entities that thrived on chaos and destruction. But this incursion hinted at something far more sinister.

'For such vile creatures to have penetrated our protective barriers meant that they were not acting alone. The presence of darker, more formidable forces loomed behind them, orchestrating this breach. These were entities of unimaginable darkness, beings whose mere existence could warp the fabric of reality. The air around us seemed to thicken with a palpable sense of dread as the enormity of our task sank in. Without a moment's hesitation, we gathered our resolve. The fight ahead would be unlike any we had faced before. The thought of confronting such powerful adversaries was daunting, but we understood the stakes. The balance between realms was teetering, and the very essence of light and goodness was at risk.

'As we raced towards the coordinates Brother David had provided, the urgency of his message echoed in our minds. Every second counted; every moment's delay could tip the scales further in favour of the encroaching darkness. We were not just racing to confront a threat but to safeguard the delicate equilibrium that held our worlds together. The clash ahead would be a battle for the soul of our existence, a fight to reclaim the light from the clutches of the abyss.

'Harry, Jack and I linked our hands, forming a triad of determination. Our minds honed in on the coordinates, the numbers burning bright in our collective consciousness. With a focused surge of energy, we willed ourselves through the ether, our bodies shimmering into being just steps away from the chaos of the battlefield.

'The air crackled with the electric intensity of combat. Smoke and the acrid scent of burning metal assaulted our senses as we blinked into existence. The ground beneath us trembled with the reverberations of distant explosions, and the sky was a rolling canvas of fire and darkness. Standing before us, amidst the tumult, was Captain Marsh, his eyes wide with a mix of relief and lingering dread. He straightened his posture, his face etched with the fatigue of relentless warfare. "Good to see you, gentlemen", he managed, his voice taut with suppressed anxiety. "We're under extreme attack by those who have been pushing the lower astrals forwards."

'As he spoke, a deafening roar shattered the air, and the ground shook violently, nearly knocking us off our feet. From behind Marsh, the battlefield erupted in a flash of crimson light, revealing shadowy figures advancing with unrelenting ferocity. Their forms flickered in and out of focus, as if they were phantoms born of the darkest nightmares, driving the astrals before them like a relentless tide.

'"We have minutes, maybe less, before they break through our defences", Marsh continued, his voice rising over the cacophony. His hand gestured toward the fortified lines where soldiers and mages alike were barely holding back the encroaching horde. "Every moment counts!"

'We nodded in unison, our breaths shallow and rapid, hearts pounding like war drums. Spiritual adrenaline surged through our veins, a fiery torrent that ignited every nerve. There was no time for hesitation or second thoughts; the moment for action had arrived, as clear and demanding as the thunderous call to arms. With fierce resolve, we drew upon the reservoirs of our mental fortitude, conjuring our intangible weapons and channelling every ounce of our energy. The air around us crackled with the intensity of our combined powers, an electric anticipation mingling with the scent of impending doom. We were preparing to plunge into the maelstrom, a swirling vortex of chaos and conflict that lay ahead.

'Before us, the scene was dire. The ground was stained with the blood of the newly slain, their bodies strewn like fallen leaves in the aftermath of a storm. Their vacant eyes, frozen in the finality of death, seemed to teeter on the brink of oblivion, awaiting a fate that hung in precarious balance. The weight of their sacrifice pressed upon us, an urgent reminder of what was at stake.

'The battle for survival had erupted with a ferocity that shook the very foundations of this place. We were thrust into its seething core, where the lines between courage and chaos blurred into a single, desperate struggle. The air was thick with the sounds of clashing steel and the cries of the wounded, an orchestral cacophony of destruction. The forces of darkness loomed ahead, a malevolent tide threatening to engulf all in its path.

'In this crucible of conflict, where the very essence of hope and despair intermingled, we stood resolute. Each heartbeat resonated with the rhythm of defiance, each breath a testament to our unyielding spirit. The fate of this place was not just at risk; it was hanging by a thread, and we were the last bulwark against its descent into the abyss. With every fibre of our beings, we surged forward, into the heart of the storm. The battle was upon us, a merciless test of our strength and resolve. We would fight, not just for ourselves, but for the flickering light of hope that yet remained. In the face of overwhelming darkness, we were the defiant flame, burning bright against the night.

'Beating the lower astrals was just frightening. As soon as we knocked them down they got up again and re-entered the fray. But over a short time we started to take away their will to fight. It was what came next that was a horror story.'

'Jim, I urgently need a break. What you are explaining in such detail is horrendous.'

Jim agreed and said he would continue the next day. I really needed to rest as my deep concentration at the computer screen had brought on a headache.

4

Out of the Darkness

An early breakfast and a cup of steaming tea by my side, I settled into my favourite chair in front of the computer. The morning light filtered softly through the window, casting a warm shadowy glow over my workspace. The gentle hum of the computer and the aromatic scent of the tea provided a comforting backdrop as I prepared to dive back into my book. My fingers hovered over the keyboard, my mind teeming with ideas and anticipation. With a deep breath, I took a sip of the hot tea, feeling its warmth seep through me, and then began typing, ready to immerse myself once more in the world I was creating.

'Jim!', I shouted mentally, scanning the dimly lit room for any sign of him. The shadows seemed to swirl and shift, playing tricks on my eyes. Out of the darkness, a voice rang out, as clear as a bell and echoing through the chamber. 'I've been here for ages.' Jim's laughter was a deep, rich sound, vibrating in the air around me, almost mocking my urgency. Relief washed over me, and I couldn't help but grin. 'Alright, I get it', I replied, my voice tinged with a mix of annoyance and amusement. 'Are you ready to start?'

Jim's form began to solidify in front of me, a faint, shimmering outline at first, then growing more defined until he stood there, as solid and real as ever. 'Now, where were we?', he asked, a mischievous glint in his eyes. 'Ah, yes, the war on the lower astral. Beating the lower astrals first – that's it.'

His expression grew serious, and a shadow crossed his face. 'The horror that follows them is something else entirely.' He paused, as if the weight of his words pressed heavily upon him. 'They were the same monsters we fought many years ago.'

Jim's eyes grew distant, as if he were peering into the past. 'It was during the Second World War, in a concentration camp. The air was thick with despair and suffering. Then, in the midst of the chaos, the Lords of Light intervened.' His voice lowered to a near whisper, charged with reverence and awe. 'If not for them, we would have succumbed to the relentless horde of demons that had entered the fray, and would have lost many new souls to them.'

The room seemed to grow colder, the very walls resonating with the memory of that ancient battle. Jim's gaze locked onto mine, the intensity of his stare almost palpable. 'The struggle was brutal. We fought tooth and nail against those vile entities, every step a fight for survival. The Lords of Light shone like beacons amidst the darkness, driving back the evil that threatened to consume us.'

I could almost see it – flashes of brilliant light clashing against shadows, the clash of powers, the cries of the fallen. The silence that followed Jim's words was heavy, filled with the echoes of a battle long past but never forgotten.

'But the war is not over', Jim continued, his voice steady yet laced with an unyielding intensity that seemed to pull the very air taut around us. His eyes, usually a window to a calm soul, now burned with an inner fire that illuminated the shadows in the room. 'Those lower astrals are still out there, lurking in the dark corners of the universe, biding their time, weaving their malevolent schemes. They are relentless, driven by an insatiable hunger to reclaim the chaos they once spread.'

Jim's words pierced the silence like a beacon of defiance. 'And we must be ready. When they rise again, we cannot falter. We must stand as one, our hearts and spirits united against the tide of darkness they will unleash.' His declaration hung in the air, a solemn vow that resonated through the fabric of reality, as if echoing across the ages and the vast expanse of the cosmos. I felt a chill run down my spine, but it was not fear. It was a resolute awakening, a sharpening of my own resolve. I nodded, my determination hardening into an unbreakable promise. No matter what lay ahead, I would etch his words into the annals of our struggle, preserving our truth as we had always done.

Jim continued: 'The adversaries we faced were more than mere phantoms or twisted reflections of humanity; they were the remnants of souls consumed by their own voracious desires, having descended into the abyss of the astral planes. Once human, these beings had become grotesque echoes of their former selves, their essence tainted and reshaped by the darkness that engulfed them. They no longer resembled anything remotely human, now existing only to serve their malevolent masters. These masters, creatures of unfathomable evil and dark ambition, were the true orchestrators of our torment. Their singular goal was to drag your world into the depths of chaos and despair, to bring hell upon earth as they had attempted before. Each clash with them had left scars both seen and unseen, yet their determination to sow destruction had never wavered. We knew their resolve, and in the face of their ceaseless plotting, our own determination had to be unbreakable.'

As Jim's voice faded, the weight of his words lingered, a haunting reminder of the battles yet to come.

'We had fought countless times before', Jim continued. 'And the path ahead promised no respite. But with each conflict, our bond grew stronger, our purpose clearer. The war was far from over, but we were ready. We would face the darkness together, standing firm against the encroaching shadows, for the sake of a future untainted by the malice of the lower astrals. Stephen, you're absolutely right. The war raged on relentlessly. Harry, Jack and I locked ourselves in a steadfast formation, a wall against any threat from behind. The stench of those abominations hung heavy in the air, their onslaught relentless and savage beyond all reckoning. The newly slain lay scattered, their lives snuffed out in an instant, unaware of the merciless force that had befallen them.

'As the newly slain struggled to rise, their bodies trembling with the aftershocks of death, a surreal haze clouded their senses. Each breath was a tentative grasp at reality, teetering on the edge of disbelief and acceptance. The very fabric of their existence felt torn between the finality of death and the unsettling awareness of an unearthly realm. Around them swirled a grotesque menagerie of horrors, each sight more nightmarish than the last. Shadows writhed and twisted into sinister forms, whispering secrets of forgotten agony. The air itself seemed heavy with the stench of decay, a tangible reminder of the boundary they had just crossed. Their minds, still reeling from the shock of mortality, struggled to comprehend the surreal landscape that unfolded before them. Faces contorted into grotesque masks of pain and terror stared back, their eyes haunted by the echoes of their own demise. Every step forward felt like wading through molasses, the weight of their newfound existence bearing down upon them with relentless force. In that moment, the boundary between life and death blurred into a haunting limbo. They were neither fully alive nor truly dead, caught in a liminal state where reality twisted and turned with each heartbeat. This was a place where the human psyche dared not tread, where the boundaries of fear and torment bled into one another, leaving them stranded in a waking nightmare from which there seemed no escape.

'As we drew closer to the two fallen soldiers, an unsettling chill ran through the air. Their eyes, wide with terror, darted around, searching for answers that weren't there. The terror etched into their faces wasn't just from the realization that they had been struck down, but from the haunting confusion that followed. They were acutely aware that something catastrophic had befallen them, yet the nature of their predicament eluded them entirely.

'In the spectral twilight, we approached, clad in uniforms that mirrored their own, a poignant reflection of the reality they were clinging to. The air was thick with tension, every step towards them feeling like a transgression into their disoriented minds. When we finally stood before them, the struggle to ask them to lay down their weapons was palpable. Their grip on their rifles was not just physical, but a desperate grasp on the last vestige of their identity and purpose.

'You might wonder: How could they still wield weapons, hold such steadfast positions when their bodies lay lifeless? It is because, in this shadowy realm between life and death, every tangible element has its ethereal counterpart. Just as their spirits lingered, tethered to the battlefield by confusion and fear, so too did their weapons exist in an astral form. These spectral arms were as much a part of them in this realm as their physical weapons were in life, a hauntingly vivid echo of their earthly existence.

'In this surreal standoff, the guns they held were not mere remnants of their military duty but symbols of their last grasp on the familiar. Their eyes, still fixed on us, flickered with a mix of fear and defiance. It was as if they were torn between the need to defend themselves and the dawning realization that such actions were futile in this liminal space. The struggle within them was almost tangible, a battle between accepting the unknown and clinging desperately to the known.

'As we gently coaxed them to lay down their spectral arms, the weight of our request pressed down on us. We weren't just asking them to release their weapons; we were asking them to let go of their last link to a world they no longer belonged to. The moment was charged with a solemn gravity, each word we spoke echoing with the unspoken truth of their new, disorienting reality.

'Suddenly, out of the swirling mist came an earsplitting screech, a sound so piercing it felt like nails clawing at our souls. It sent chills racing down our spines, forewarning of the horrors about to emerge. From the dense fog, the lower astrals surged forth – twisted, shadowy figures with hollow eyes that seemed to suck the light from the air. They attacked us with a visceral malevolence, their howls blending into a cacophony of madness.

'The newly slain amongst us, wide-eyed and trembling, reflexively raised their rifles and unleashed a volley of bullets. Each shot passed harmlessly through the spectral forms, vanishing into the mist with a faint whimper. Panic gripped the freshly dead, their faces paling as the reality of their futility struck them like a physical blow. Their hands shook violently, the weapons falling from their grasp as they backed away in horror, unable to comprehend the phantoms they faced.

'Harry, Jack and I moved swiftly, our actions honed by countless battles against these otherworldly abominations. We engaged the astrals with grim determination, our mental weapons of light slicing through the fog, dispersing the spectral assailants one by one. But as we carved our way through the ethereal onslaught, a deeper shadow loomed behind the throng of lesser entities. A presence far more insidious stirred within the mist, its darkness deeper and more oppressive than the astrals we had just vanquished.

'As the last of the screeching apparitions dissolved into the void, a silence fell, thick and suffocating. Then, from the heart of the fog, it emerged. A figure, colossal and grotesque, materialized slowly, its form undulating as if not fully solid. Eyes like black abysses glowed with a cold, malevolent intelligence, and a mouth full of jagged teeth curled into a chilling grin. The air around it seemed to warp and bend, the temperature plummeting as its presence sucked the warmth from our surroundings.

'This was no mere astral entity. It was a nightmare made flesh, a horror dredged up from the deepest pits of the beyond. Its gaze fixed on us, and for a moment time seemed to freeze, locking us in a silent, breathless standoff with the embodiment of pure dread.

'"God!" At that moment Jack's voice cracked as he let out a cry that echoed through the mist. "What in God's name is that?"

'Over the countless battles we had fought together, our group had confronted some truly dreadful apparitions – ghastly entities so dark and malevolent that merely laying eyes on them had made me feel spiritually ill. Yet this monstrosity was unlike anything we had ever encountered. Its grotesque form seemed to warp reality itself, bending the light around it into a suffocating shroud of despair. My blood ran cold, and a visceral sense of dread clawed at my heart, threatening to suffocate me. In a panic, I reached out with my mind, sending a desperate plea for aid to Brother David. "We need your help – no, we need a miracle."'

'"We are coming." Brother David's response was immediate, his voice a beacon of hope cutting through the oppressive darkness. The creature before us was an abomination, a nightmare made from the etheric atoms of the plane it was born in. Its twisted body pulsed with a malevolent energy, and its eyes, or what could be called eyes, glowed with a fiery malice that seared into our souls. Any poor soul, newly slain or otherwise, who gazed upon this horror would surely be stricken with such profound terror that death would be a mercy. I could feel its malevolence wrapping around us like a cold, clammy fog, suffocating our will to fight.

'The stench of decay and the acrid scent of burnt flesh filled the air, mingling with the fear that hung like a shroud over us. I glanced at Jack, his face pale and drawn, his eyes wide with horror. For a moment, the weight of our situation pressed down upon me like a crushing wave. The mist seemed to close in, the darkness pressing against us from all sides as the creature advanced, its gnarled claws scraping against the ground with a sound that set my teeth on edge. I felt a cold sweat break out across my brow, my heart hammering in my chest. We had faced many horrors before, but nothing could have prepared us for this.'

'"Hold fast!" Brother David's voice rang out in my mind, a lifeline in the storm. "We will face this together."

'With renewed determination, the three of us stood our ground, creating a mental shield around us all. The battle ahead would be unlike any we had fought before, but we would not face it alone. The creature's assault began with a ferocity that shook us to our core. Its monstrous form surged forward, ripping through our defenses with relentless fury. Each blow it struck sent shockwaves of fear through our ranks. Yet, despite the overwhelming power and the gnashing of teeth that threatened to consume us all, we clung to our positions, our resolve unyielding. But our mental barricades buckled under the creature's might, the very air around us quaking with its roars. Each impact of its fists was a brutal reminder of the monstrous force we faced. The ground beneath us seemed to tremble in resonance with the beast's fury, and the echoes of our defiant cries mixed with the cacophony of battle.

'As our strength began to wane and the hope of survival dimmed, a clarion call rang out over the din of the struggle. Through the haze of dust and debris, Brother David emerged, a beacon of resolve and salvation. His arrival was not solitary; behind him surged a wave of reinforcements, their determined faces reflecting the fire of a shared purpose. They moved like a tide, bolstering our faltering lines and breathing new life into our fight. With Brother David at the helm, we found a renewed strength, a spark of hope igniting in the darkness of our desperation.

'Immediately, Brother David found himself face-to-face with the towering demonic entity, its eyes glowing like embers of hellfire. The air crackled with an oppressive energy, the very essence of malevolence seemed to seep from its every pore. The creature's claws were like razors, its breath a sulphurous wind. But Brother David stood his ground, unwavering; his heart a fortress of faith amidst the storm of fear that raged around him.

'With a deep breath, Brother David steeled himself, feeling the weight of his crucifix against his chest. He closed his eyes, shutting out the demonic visage before him, and focused inward. He called upon every ounce of strength he possessed, reaching deep into the wellspring of his soul. The words of ancient prayers began to form on his lips, each syllable a beacon of light piercing through the darkness that enveloped him. "Lord, grant me your strength", he whispered, his voice growing louder with each word, transforming from a tremble to a roar. "By the power of the Holy Spirit, deliver us from this evil!"

'As he spoke, Brother David felt a surge of divine power coursing through his veins, a holy fire igniting within him. It spread from his heart to his fingertips, a blazing light that pushed back against the encroaching shadows. He thrust his hands forward, palms outstretched, as if to cast the darkness back into the abyss from which it came. The demonic entity recoiled, its snarls turning to hisses of pain as the light emanating from David began to envelop it. The ground beneath them trembled, and a brilliant radiance spread everywhere, pushing the darkness to the edges. With every word of prayer, Brother David's voice became a thunderous command, echoing with the authority of a thousand angels.

'"In the name of the Father, the Son, and the Holy Spirit", he declared, his voice echoing with a power that was not his own, "I cast you out!"

'The creature let out a final, ear-piercing shriek as the holy light engulfed it completely, its form dissolving into wisps of black smoke. The oppressive energy that had filled the battle ground dissipated, leaving behind a serene silence. Brother David fell to his knees, breathless and trembling, but triumphant. The battle was won, not by his strength alone, but by the unwavering faith that had lit his path through the darkest of nights.

'In the chilling shadows of the battlefield, where every heartbeat echoes with the thud of distant artillery and the air is thick with the acrid scent of smoke and blood, lurk insidious entities. These malevolent beings thrive on more than just the chaos of war; they feed on the very essence of human suffering. They are drawn to fear like moths to a flame, their existence a cruel parasitic dance around the agony of the living. Every flicker of dread in a soldier's eyes, every tremor of uncertainty in their stance, is like nectar to these dark forces. They revel in the silent cries of those whose courage falters. For each drop of pain, whether it's the searing physical torment of a wound or the harrowing emotional burden of loss and despair, these entities grow stronger, more formidable.

'On this grim stage, where courage is tested to its limits and every man and woman bears the scars of their own personal battles, no one is immune. Pain is the universal currency of this hellish theatre, a shared burden that etches lines into the faces of even the bravest. Whether it's the raw sting of a fresh injury, the gnawing ache of exhaustion, or the invisible wounds that carve deep into the soul, every soldier is a reservoir of agony. The two soldiers we helped were a shimmering wreck on seeing the sight of pure evil. They were quickly taken away to a place of adjustment.

'As the war rages on, Stephen, the battlefield becomes a feeding ground for these insidious creatures. They weave through the ranks, invisible to the eye but ever-present, siphoning strength from the misery that envelops them. The bravest cries of defiance, the whispered prayers for survival, and the silent, steely resolve of the combatants all become tainted by the pervasive spectre of these fear-mongers. In this crucible of conflict, it is not just the physical struggle that determines fate, but the internal war against despair. For every soldier, the fight is as much against these unseen parasites as it is against the tangible enemy before them. They are the true adversaries, lurking in the recesses of the mind, waiting to feast on the inevitable sorrow and suffering that war so cruelly delivers.'

5

Embrace of Heaven

I couldn't have foreseen the profound impact Jim's words would have on me. When he spoke yesterday, a chill ran down my spine, his voice carrying an almost ethereal weight that lingered in the air. His perspective on the afterlife was unlike anything I had encountered before.

Most people I had spoken with about death and what comes after held a comforting, almost simplistic belief: that upon our last breath, we are welcomed into the warm embrace of heaven. It's a thought that offers solace and a sense of peace, a straight path to eternal bliss. That was until I penned my first book, *Seven Steps To Eternity*.

But Jim's words were different. They weren't just about the destination; they delved into the very essence of the journey, painting a picture that was both haunting and beautiful. He spoke of realms and transitions, of the soul's voyage through unseen dimensions before it reaches its final resting place. His description was so vivid, so filled with passion and conviction, that it stirred something deep within me, something I didn't even know was there.

His narrative seemed to unravel the fabric of my understanding, leaving me questioning everything I had taken for granted about life and what lies beyond. It was as if Jim had opened a door to a mysterious world, one that beckoned me with both fear and fascination. The certainty with which others had spoken of heaven now felt like a fragile construct, easily shattered by the depth and complexity of Jim's vision.

In that moment, as I absorbed his words, I felt a profound shift within me – a realization that the afterlife is not just a destination but a vast, intricate journey that each soul embarks upon. It was a realization that would linger with me, reshaping my thoughts and beliefs in ways I could never have imagined.

I sat at my computer, the glow of the screen casting a soft light over my cluttered desk. A hot cup of tea sat steaming beside me, the aroma of Earl Grey mingling with the comforting scent of buttered toast. This morning ritual was my sanctuary, a quiet prelude to the day's writing.

As I prepared to delve into my manuscript, I anticipated the familiar, ghostly slap on my shoulder – Jim's playful signal that he was here, ready to join me in our literary endeavours. But today the air was charged with an unexpected presence, different from the usual ethereal nudge. Instead of Jim's reassuring touch, I felt a chill ripple down my spine.

'Good morning', a voice boomed, breaking the morning's silence like a thunderclap. Startled, I turned to find not Jim, but Harry, standing with an imposing yet cordial presence. His figure seemed to shimmer slightly, as if not entirely part of this world, yet his eyes were vivid, alive with stories untold.

'Jim sends his apologies', Harry continued, his voice a deep, resonant echo that filled the room. 'He said he'll be here as soon as he finishes his rest period.'

'Well', I stammered, struggling to mask my surprise. 'This is – unexpected. I've heard so much about you and Jack from Jim. It's a pleasure to finally meet you, Harry. I didn't realize you needed rest too?'

Harry's laugh was a rumble, both haunting and human. 'Oh yes', he replied, his expression softening into something almost wistful. 'Even though we have passed over, we still carry the weight of our human experiences. The stench of war – it lingers in our souls, affecting us in ways you might not imagine. We are, after all, still beings with our own set of emotions.'

The room seemed to dim around his words, as if the shadows of his memories seeped into the air. I imagined the scenes he had witnessed, the horrors that haunted his rest.

Harry continued, his voice now a gentle murmur. 'We may not have flesh and bone, but our spirits remember. We need time to process, to recover from the echoes of our past. Just like you.' I nodded slowly, feeling a newfound respect for the unseen toll on my spectral companions. The room felt heavier, laden with the gravity of Harry's revelation. But alongside that weight, there was a profound sense of connection – a bridge between our worlds, built on shared struggles and the enduring human spirit.

'Thank you for telling me', I said quietly. 'I hadn't realized. It makes me appreciate your company even more.'

Harry smiled, a brief flicker of light in the dim room. 'And we appreciate yours', he replied. 'Now, let's get to work. Jim will be here soon enough.'

As I turned back to my computer, the keys felt different under my fingers. The day's writing awaited, but now, with the presence of Harry, it was imbued with a deeper purpose. The stories we would create together were not just about the past, but a tribute to the resilience of the human soul – alive or otherwise.

'First', Harry began, his voice steady and calm, 'let me explain how we find our rest. Unlike humans, who need sleep to rejuvenate their bodies and minds, we operate differently. Instead of sleep, we turn to meditation. This isn't just any ordinary meditation – it's a deep, profound practice that allows us to reach into the very core of our being. Through this, we connect with the universal flow of energy that permeates all existence, drawing from it to replenish ourselves.'

Harry's eyes seemed to glow with an inner light as he spoke, the intensity of his words filling the room. 'But that's not all. We've been trained to cleanse our energy fields with nothing more than our thoughts. Imagine this: your mind acting as a powerful broom, sweeping away the dust and debris that accumulate in your soul. Every negative emotion, every dark thought, every residue from the battles we fight – it's all wiped clean with a mere flicker of intent.'

He paused, letting the weight of his words settle, then continued with a hint of a smile. 'After cleansing, we don't stop there. We then focus our thoughts on recharging, drawing in the purest, most vibrant energies from the cosmos. It's like basking in the rays of the sun, but these rays don't just warm your skin – they penetrate deep into your essence, revitalizing every part of you.'

Harry leaned forward, his voice taking on a more intimate tone. 'But sometimes, even that isn't enough. There are moments when the weight of our battles becomes too much, and we need more than just meditation and thought to recover. That's when we retreat to a sanctuary – a place far removed from the chaos of the battlefield. There, in the company of kindred spirits, we find solace and strength.'

He closed his eyes briefly, as if picturing the place he spoke of. 'On our own plane of existence, we have what we call the Power Pools. These pools are hidden gems, secret havens that only a few know about. Imagine stepping into a body of water that isn't just liquid, but pure energy in a tangible form. As you immerse yourself, you feel every inch of your being come alive. It's as if the very essence of life is embracing you, infusing you with an overwhelming sense of peace and vitality.'

Harry's gaze sharpened, locking onto his audience with a fierce intensity. 'In these pools, we don't need any mystical imagery or elaborate rituals to recharge. The moment we enter, we are enveloped in a symphony of energies, each note resonating with our deepest frequencies. It's an experience beyond words, beyond comprehension – a direct communion with the forces that sustain us. By simply being in these pools, we are renewed; our strength restored completely.'

He leaned back, a look of deep satisfaction on his face. 'So you see, while our methods may differ from what you know, they are no less effective. Whether through meditation, the power of our thoughts, or the profound embrace of the Power Pools, we find our rest and gather the strength we need to continue our journey.'

The room was silent, I was lost in the vivid imagery and profound truths Harry had shared. For a moment, it was as if we too could feel the serene energy of the Power Pools, our souls resonating with the possibility of such a wondrous experience.

Harry delved deeper into the mysteries of the afterlife, his voice carrying the weight of profound realization. 'Imagine', he began, 'that all human beings are like sponges, absorbing every ounce of thought energy around them. It doesn't matter whether this energy is beneficial or harmful; we take it all in without discretion. This unseen influence shapes our very essence, often without our awareness.'

He paused, his eyes reflecting the depth of his understanding. 'Picture the myriad of thoughts that bombard us daily', he continued, 'from the whispers of joy and hope to the shadows of despair and anger. We are constantly submerged in an ocean of these energies. Just like sponges, we soak up everything, regardless of its nature. It's a relentless process, occurring beneath the surface of our consciousness.'

Harry's expression grew more intense, his passion evident. 'This absorption has consequences. The good thoughts nourish us, fostering growth and positivity. But the dark, negative energies? They seep into our souls, clouding our minds and burdening our spirits. It's a silent, almost insidious invasion that we often overlook.'

He leaned forward, his voice dropping to a whisper as if sharing a sacred secret. 'In the afterlife, this exchange becomes even more profound. Spirits, unbound by physical limitations, are even more susceptible to these energies. They exist in a realm where thought and emotion are potent forces, capable of transcending boundaries we cannot yet comprehend.'

Harry's gaze was unwavering, filled with a mixture of awe and caution. 'Understanding this', he concluded, 'is crucial. For it is not just our physical selves that are shaped by the energies we absorb, but our very souls. And in the realms beyond, where thought is reality, the stakes are infinitely higher.'

With that, Harry fell silent. His words had not merely extended his knowledge; they had opened a window into the profound and often unseen forces that influence all existence. His eyes twinkled with a blend of mischief and deep understanding as he glanced up, the faintest hint of a smile playing on his lips. 'Ha, I've just received a message from Jim', he announced, his voice barely more than a whisper, yet carrying the weight of profound significance. 'He's asked me to continue guiding you', he added, his tone reverent, 'because his mentor, Chan, has tasked him with a vital endeavour – one that delves into fortifying Jim's resilience.'

Harry paused, his gaze drifting into the ethereal distance as if peering through the veils of the spirit realm itself. 'You see', he continued, his voice now a resonant echo, filled with an otherworldly wisdom, 'in this boundless expanse we call the spirit world, our journey of learning is eternal. We are ceaseless seekers of knowledge, even in our moments of rest and reflection. This place, while serene, is also a crucible where we forge the strength of our souls.'

He leaned in closer, his eyes gleaming with an intensity that seemed to pierce the fabric of reality. 'Our ability to manifest our deepest fantasies here is astonishing, almost limitless', he murmured, his voice carrying a sense of awe and caution. 'But these creations can be capricious, their stability as fleeting as a whisper on the wind. That is why we are endlessly taught the art of control – how to master our thoughts and desires, to prevent them from spiralling into chaos.'

Harry's gaze softened, a compassionate warmth replacing the earlier intensity. 'It is a delicate balance we strive to maintain', he said softly, 'for in this realm, our inner world becomes our outer reality. And so, Jim's journey now is one of great importance. He must learn to temper his inner storms and harness the incredible power within him. Just as you must.'

He straightened, the momentary solemnity giving way to a gentle smile. 'So, here we are', he concluded, his voice a reassuring balm. 'You and I, continuing on this path of discovery and growth.

Together, we shall navigate the wonders and challenges of this spirit world, ever learning, ever evolving.' Harry's speech was imbued with a sense of gravitas and depth, highlighting the continuous learning process in the spirit world and the delicate balance between fantasy and control.

'When you first penned *Seven Steps to Eternity*, perhaps you did not fully grasp the monumental impact your words would wield. You embarked on a literary voyage, guiding readers through the mystical expanses of the astral plane, detailing a profound journey of souls that transcend the physical realm. Little did you know that your creation would become a beacon of enlightenment and transformation for countless individuals. This book has not merely entertained; it has ignited sparks of hope, offered solace and paved paths to profound self-discovery. Your narrative has whispered to the very essence of the human spirit, rekindling faith in the unseen and inspiring a reawakening to the possibilities beyond our material existence. Many have found their lives irrevocably uplifted and reshaped, finding purpose and peace in the ethereal truths your words have unveiled. Indeed, *Seven Steps to Eternity* has woven itself into the fabric of their lives, guiding them toward a horizon where the eternal and the temporal dance in sublime harmony.

'As we embark on the creation of this book, we are weaving together a tapestry of thoughts and revelations that will resonate deeply with those who seek to traverse the ethereal pathways of the spirit realm. This book is not merely a collection of words but a gateway to profound understanding for those whose souls are stirred by the mystical and the unseen. It promises to touch the hearts and minds of seekers who yearn for a deeper, more transcendent connection with the spiritual forces that shape our existence. Prepare to journey beyond the veil, where the whispers of the universe will guide you to a higher plane of enlightenment and wonder.

'Now, Stephen', Harry declared with a hint of defiance dancing in his eyes and a wry smirk playing on his lips. His voice carried the weight of hard-earned wisdom. 'Let me paint for you the haunting portrait of a soldier's existence amidst the horrors of the First World War. Imagine a world where the sun itself seemed hesitant to pierce the thick veil of smoke that hung perpetually over the desolate battlefields. The air was thick with the acrid tang of gunpowder and the metallic bite of blood – a symphony of suffering that resonated through every trench and every shattered soul.'

His gaze turned inward for a moment, as if reliving the scenes etched into his memory. 'In those trenches, life was stripped down to its rawest form – a relentless ballet of survival and sacrifice. The days blurred into nights, each passing hour etching lines of weariness and resolve into faces too young to carry such burdens. We fought not just against the enemy but against the very essence of despair that threatened to engulf us.'

Harry's voice lowered, weighted with solemnity. 'It was a world where innocence was shattered like glass, where camaraderie was forged in the crucible of shared hardship and fleeting moments of humanity amidst the carnage. Every step through the mud, every heartbeat drowned out by the thunder of artillery, was a testament to the resilience of the human spirit and the grim reality of war.'

He paused, his eyes meeting mine with a mixture of defiance and sorrow. 'The life of a First World War soldier was not just a chapter in history – it was a saga of courage and sacrifice that echoes through time, a stark reminder of the depths of darkness humanity can endure and the indomitable strength that can emerge from its crucible.'

Suddenly, a forceful slap thundered against my back, jolting me from my thoughts. 'I'm here', Jim declared, his voice slicing through the tense silence that had enveloped us. 'Looks like Harry's been keeping you out of trouble.' His laughter boomed across the room, mingling with Harry's own chuckles.

'One of these days, Jim, you'll send me straight to the grave with your entrances', I exclaimed breathlessly, my heart pounding in my chest. 'I'm not ready to venture into the spirit world just yet. Not now, not when we still have the book to finish.' I glanced at Harry for confirmation, seeking reassurance in his nod.

'Exactly', Harry affirmed solemnly, his gaze flickering between Jim and me, his voice resonating with unwavering determination. 'The book comes first. You're not crossing over until it's done. Understand, Stephen?'

My eyes sparked with mischievous intent, but I quickly composed myself, adopting a serious demeanour as I nodded in agreement. 'Alright, alright. The book it is then.'

'But remember', Jim interjected, his tone tinged with urgency, 'time is not on your side. We must finish what we started before it's too late.'

'What? Am I to meet my end soon?', I queried with a mix of curiosity and apprehension.

'No, not yet', Jim reassured, his voice steady. 'But when your time comes, we'll be here, ready to welcome you to your new home.'

The room fell into a heavy silence once more, the weight of our task settling around us like a suffocating shroud. In that moment, we understood the gravity of our mission. Together, with resolve etched into our hearts, we were determined to see this through, undeterred by the challenges ahead or the unexpected twists Jim might throw our way.

With a solemn nod and a faint smile, Harry bid his farewells, his voice tinged with a hint of reluctance. 'I've truly enjoyed our time together', he murmured, his gaze lingering momentarily. 'But now', he sighed, 'duty calls. I must return to my work on the astral plane.' His words hung in the air, laden with unspoken promises of future encounters and adventures beyond mortal realms.

'I see Harry has been delving into the First World War with you', Jim remarked, his voice carrying a weight of sombre reflection. 'In my talks I delved deeply into the profound experiences of dying and awakening in the astral plane. War, any war, embodies those harrowing moments where the living and the dying find themselves caught in a whirlwind of chaos and uncertainty. Death, that abrupt and merciless force, severs the ties to the physical form in an instant. Yet the essence of who we are persists, albeit in a surreal transformation – the astral body a ghostly echo of our former selves.

'Imagine, if you will, the disorientation of consciousness suddenly thrust into a realm beyond comprehension. Thoughts and emotions remain intact, clinging stubbornly to the remnants of life left behind. It's a liminal space where reality bends and perceptions blur. The battlefield becomes a stage where souls, severed from flesh but not from identity, wander in disbelief and anguish.

'All wars are chapters in this tragic narrative, where the lines between life and death blur into a haunting continuum. The fallen, unaware of their transition, linger in a twilight existence, grappling with the profound dissonance of their altered state. It's a testament to the enduring spirit, resilient yet shattered, navigating realms where the laws of existence bend to unknown forces. So yes, Harry's exploration into the First World War brings to light these profound truths – the stark realities of life's fragility and the haunting persistence of the human spirit amidst the chaos of war.'

Jim's words struck me with the force of a meteorite hurtling through the atmosphere, shattering the tranquil stillness of our conversation. They resonated within me like a seismic tremor, awakening a dormant curiosity that demanded satisfaction.

'How do wars start?', Jim asked. His question hung in the air like a dense fog, enveloping me in its weighty significance. In that moment, the room seemed to fade away, replaced by a vast tableau of history's most turbulent chapters. Images of battles and conflicts flashed before my mind's eye, each one a testament to the complexities of human strife. The echoes of past declarations, betrayals and alliances reverberated through my thoughts, weaving a tapestry of causes and consequences that shaped nations and destinies.

I found myself grappling with the enormity of his inquiry, searching for clarity amidst the tangled web of politics, ideologies and power struggles. It was as if Jim's question had opened a Pandora's box of historical narratives, each revealing a piece of the puzzle that defined the nature of conflict.

With each passing moment, the urgency of his words intensified, compelling me to delve deeper into the annals of warfare. I was driven by an insatiable thirst for understanding, propelled forward by the gravity of his question that demanded not just an answer, but an exploration of the very fabric of human nature itself.

As I sat there, immersed in contemplation, I realized that Jim's question was not merely a quest for knowledge; it was a profound reflection on the fragile balance between peace and discord, unity and division. It challenged me to confront the complexities of human behaviour and the myriad forces that propel societies towards conflict.

In that moment, I understood that the quest for peace begins with the understanding of war. Jim's words had ignited a fire within me – a quest for insight, a journey through history's corridors to unravel the tangled roots of conflict. And as I embarked on this intellectual odyssey, I knew that his question would linger with me, driving me onward in pursuit of a deeper understanding of the world we inhabit.

Jim broke my concentration. 'Your perspective is fascinating, but the truth runs far deeper than meets the eye. The insatiable hunger for power acts as a magnet, pulling towards it the entities from the boundless expanse of the astral plane. It's a cosmic dance governed by the immutable Law of Attraction, where intentions become threads weaving through the fabric of existence. Forces beyond mortal comprehension are stirred, their unseen tendrils reaching out to intertwine with human ambition, shaping destinies and forging alliances that span realms unknown. This nexus of desires and energies forms a tapestry of intricacy and consequence, where every thought, action and aspiration resonates beyond the tangible, echoing across dimensions in a symphony of cosmic influence.'

'So what are you saying?', I asked him nervously.

'Many of your leaders are weak, frail in both resolve and spirit', Jim stated with sense of disdain. 'They cloak themselves in the garb of authority and wisdom, masquerading as stewards of your future, yet beneath this veneer lies a sinister reality. Their smiles may be polished and their speeches eloquent, but don't be deceived. These men and women who hold the reins of power, harbour agendas far darker and more insidious than you can fathom.

'Behind closed doors, they conspire, weaving webs of deceit and manipulation. They are not just tainted by the common stains of greed and ambition; they are profoundly and irredeemably corrupt. Their hearts are blackened by a moral decay that permeates their every action. But it goes deeper than mere immorality – there is a spiritual rot at their core, a corruption that festers in their very souls.

'Yes, before you even ask, Stephen, they are spiritually corrupt! Their spirits are tainted, twisted by their relentless pursuit of power and control. They feign righteousness and piety, all the while their souls wither under the weight of their duplicity. They are the architects of despair, the harbingers of a future devoid of hope and light.

'Beware these false shepherds who lead their flocks astray. For in their hearts lies a void where virtue should dwell, replaced instead by an abyss of malevolence and deceit. They are the puppeteers of your destiny, pulling the strings from the shadows, and every decision they make, every law they pass, is but another stitch in the shroud they weave around your freedoms and your dreams. They are the dark shadows in your halls of power, the silent saboteurs of your liberty. And unless you awaken to their true nature, you will find yourselves ensnared in a fate dictated not by the common good, but by their insidious designs. The hour is late, but the truth must be faced: your leaders are not just flawed, they are the very embodiment of corruption and spiritual decay.

'Many of those in positions of power and influence are not merely guided by their own intentions and decisions. They are, in fact, encircled by lower astral beings – entities that lurk in the unseen realms just beyond the veil of your physical reality. These entities, make no mistake, possess a cunning and profound intelligence. Their role is to insidiously attach themselves to the aura of the powerful, acting as invisible puppeteers who subtly steer these individuals towards paths that align with darker, more malevolent forces. These astral entities are masters of manipulation, whispering in the ears of leaders, subtly bending their will to serve the agenda of negativity and discord. The course they chart is often one fraught with peril and corruption, leading societies into chaos and decay. It is not mere coincidence that we see conflicts erupt, societies unravel, and injustices perpetuate; these are the manifestations of unseen hands at work.

'Now, prepare yourself for a revelation that may shake your very core. The figure you know as the Antichrist, often depicted as a singular, malevolent being destined to bring about the end times, is not one person. In reality, this dark force has fragmented into three distinct entities. Each of these entities exists within your world today, wielding influence in ways that shape the destiny of mankind. These three figures, embodying the essence of the Antichrist, are dispersed across different spheres of power. They act as harbingers of the same insidious force, orchestrating events and manipulating human actions to serve their ominous purpose. Each one thrives in an environment that amplifies their dark agenda, be it in the corridors of political power, the towers of economic control, or the realms of ideological dominance.

'In recognizing this, we must open our eyes to the multifaceted nature of the threats we face. The Antichrist is not merely a figure of folklore or apocalyptic prophecy but a real and present danger, manifested through these three influential entities that walk among you. It is a call to awareness, to vigilance and to the understanding that the battle against these forces is not only a spiritual or symbolic one but a tangible struggle for the very soul of your world. You cannot get near to those people as they are guarded by lower astral beings.'

'Yes, Jim', I replied. 'I fully understand where you're coming from. I feel the weight of your words and the storm of disillusionment they bring. The landscape we're looking at is bleak – an endless horizon marred by the shadows of those who abuse their power and betray the trust of the very people they are meant to serve. But here's what troubles me to the core: amidst this sea of corruption, there are still those rare souls, those noble individuals, who cling to their principles, striving to lead with honour and integrity. How do they navigate this treacherous terrain?'

'Imagine the internal turmoil they must endure each day', Jim stated, 'waking up with the intention to do good, to make a difference, only to find themselves surrounded by deceit and malfeasance. How do they follow leaders who mock the very essence of justice and morality? How do they stand in the council chambers, the meeting rooms, the corridors of power, where every whisper and every action seems tainted by corruption?

'Picture them, Stephen – these uncorrupted few – as they walk through the corridors of power, their hearts heavy with the knowledge that they are but islands of integrity in a vast ocean of deceit. Every decision they make is a tightrope walk, a delicate balance between their duty and their conscience. How do they reconcile the contradiction of following leaders who erode the foundations of everything they believe in?

'Consider the courage it must take for them to voice dissent, knowing that their voices are often drowned out by the cacophony of lies and self-interest. How do they resist the seductive pull of complicity, the ease of turning a blind eye, when the cost of standing firm could mean isolation or even ruin?

'Stephen, it's more than just a battle against external corruption; it's a constant war within their souls. Each day, they must confront the grim reality that their ideals are at odds with the actions of those above them. They must ask themselves: can they remain true to their values while following leaders who embody everything they oppose?

'It's a harrowing journey, one that tests the limits of their endurance and the depth of their commitment to justice. How do they muster the strength to continue, to not let the pervasive darkness extinguish their light? How do they preserve their own sense of self, their integrity, when every step they take is mired in the filth of corruption?

'And yet, despite the overwhelming odds, some do persevere. They fight, not just for their own souls, but for the hope that someday, their steadfastness might spark a change, however small. They hold onto the belief that their actions, their refusal to succumb to the rot around them, might inspire others to rise up and reclaim the dignity and honour that have been so gravely tarnished. In the face of such despair, it's this sliver of hope, this relentless pursuit of a higher standard, that drives them. But the question remains: How long can they endure the shadows before even their light is consumed?'

Jim continued, his voice tinged with a mix of fervour and melancholy: 'They say that money corrupts, but I must disagree. Money, in its essence, is neutral – a mere tool, a vessel without will or moral compass. It's the hands that wield it, the intentions behind its use, that determine its nature. There is no such thing as bad money, only those who bend it to their own sinister purposes.

'Look around you, see how the corridors of power are lined not just with opulence but with the whispers of deals made in shadows, decisions brokered behind closed doors. Do you not see the pattern? Most senators of the American Congress step into their roles with modest means, barely scraping into the upper echelons of wealth. And yet, when they leave, they emerge as millionaires, their fortunes mysteriously multiplied many times over.

'Ask yourself how? How is it that these men and women, sworn to serve the public, can amass such wealth in the span of a few years? It's not through their salaries alone – that much is clear. The official pay-check of a senator, while respectable, is hardly the path to a vast fortune. No, it's something far more insidious.

'Consider the ways in which influence and affluence intertwine in the dark dance of politics. Think about the lobbyists who linger in the wings, offering lucrative "consulting" roles and "speaking" fees. Reflect on the countless "investments" and "stock options" that find their way into the hands of those who have the power to make or break legislation. These aren't coincidences, Stephen – they are calculated moves in a game where the stakes are power and control, not just over money, but over the lives of millions.

'Picture this: a senator enters the hallowed halls of Congress, perhaps with noble intentions, a desire to make a difference. But soon, they are swept up in the whirlwind of influence, peddling and backdoor negotiations. They start to see how easily fortunes are made, not through hard work or innovation, but through leveraging their position and selling pieces of their soul.

'Think of the temptations they face daily, the subtle and not-so-subtle offers of wealth in exchange for their loyalty to corporate interests or the political machine. It starts with a simple favour, a small vote in a committee, but it spirals into a web of entanglements, where each thread is lined with gold.

'How do they resist? How do they maintain their integrity when every corner turned offers another opportunity to trade their principles for profit? Some might start with the best of intentions, but slowly, inevitably, they are drawn into the abyss of greed and self-interest. And those who refuse to play the game? They are marginalized, sidelined or quietly pushed out. The system, as it stands, rewards those who succumb, who are willing to sacrifice their duty to the public for personal gain. It punishes those who dare to remain unyielding, who cling to the belief that they can serve without being seduced by wealth. Do you not see, Stephen? It's a cycle of corruption, perpetuated not by money itself, but by the insatiable hunger for more – the relentless pursuit of wealth that overrides any sense of justice or honour. The problem is not the money, but the moral decay that it reveals in those who are entrusted with power. It's a tragic irony that those who are meant to protect you from corruption often become its most ardent practitioners.

'As we watch these senators transform from modest servants to affluent power-brokers, we must ask ourselves: How many of them have traded their integrity for riches? How many have compromised their duty to the people for the allure of a fattened bank account? The answer, I fear, is too many.'

Jim leaned forward, his eyes glinting with a mix of fear and determination as he continued his tale. 'You think America is unique in its corruption?', he asked, his voice barely above a whisper, yet heavy with the weight of dark secrets. 'No, my friend. The rot runs deep and wide, crossing oceans and continents. This is not just about money or power. What we are witnessing is far more insidious, a plot so sinister that it unfolds right in front of you, hidden in plain sight.'

He paused, scanning the room, as if gauging whether he should continue elaborating on the words he had just uttered. It was safe to proceed. His gaze lingered on my face, searching for signs of disbelief or the strength to hear more.

'The puppet masters, those who control the strings of your so-called civilized nations, are engaged in something so diabolical, it chills the blood. Their machinations are beyond mere political manoeuvring or economic domination. It's something darker, something that strikes at the very heart of humanity.' Jim's voice trembled slightly, a testament to the gravity of his words.

'Children!' The word tore from his lips, drenched in disgust, his voice trembling with barely contained fury. 'Children are the heart of their monstrous scheme, the very core of their despicable conspiracy. It's a horror so profound, so unthinkable, that I can scarcely bring myself to speak of it. The most grotesque part? Powerful women, up to their necks in this depravity, some even mothers themselves! They betray their own flesh and blood, perpetuating this barbaric cruelty with a coldness that chills the soul.'

Jim fell silent, the air thick with a mixture of curiosity and dread. Jim's eyes pleaded for understanding, yet begged not to be pushed further. 'Please', he implored, his voice barely a whisper now, 'don't ask me to reveal more. For your own sake, don't dig deeper. Some truths are too horrifying to confront.'

He leaned back, the fire in his eyes dimming, replaced by a haunted look. The weight of the secrets he held seemed to age him in that instant. The room remained silent. I was grappling with the unspoken horrors Jim had hinted at, and the chilling realization that some truths might be better left buried.

'What I will tell you is this', he declared, his eyes blazing with an unyielding fire. 'No evil deed escapes the relentless grip of Justice. Those who perpetuate these heinous crimes – these vile atrocities against innocence – will soon discover a harsh and immutable truth. No fortress of wealth, no castle built on their ill-gotten gains, will shield them from the inexorable law of cause and effect. Their riches, their power, will crumble to dust in the face of retribution. They will come to understand, far too late, that the universe exacts a terrible price from those who sow such seeds of wickedness. Their judgment day is coming, and no amount of gold can buy them reprieve from the reckoning that awaits.

'I think I would like to end it there for today, Stephen, and I will be with you tomorrow.'

With those final, enigmatic words, Jim abruptly departed, his exit as sudden as his statement was mysterious. I sat there, stunned and bewildered, his cryptic expression echoing in my mind like an unsolved riddle. The air seemed heavy with the weight of his unspoken meaning.

Unable to shake off the intrigue, I retreated to my computer after dinner, hoping to find some semblance of clarity. My curiosity about what Jim was alluding to consumed me. His cryptic hints lingered in my mind, refusing to let go. I became obsessed, compelled to understand the hidden truths he was so subtly pointing towards. The internet became my hunting ground. I plunged into its darkest depths, navigating through obscure forums, anonymous threads and shadowy websites, piecing together every fragment of information I could find.

Each discovery felt like a punch to the gut. The deeper I delved, the more grotesque and horrifying the revelations became. It was as if I had peeled back the layers of a benign world to uncover a festering underbelly of unimaginable depravity and corruption. With every click, my stomach churned, and a sense of dread gripped me tighter. I found myself gasping for breath as the sheer weight of what I was uncovering bore down on me.

I cannot, in good conscience, divulge the specifics of what I unearthed. The content is too vile, too unsettling to be mentioned casually here. To recount what I found would not only be a disservice to you but also a betrayal of the innocuous facade that our everyday reality hides.

6

New Beginnings

As the first rays of dawn began to seep through the curtains, their warm glow gently coaxed me from the remnants of my slumber. The morning had arrived in all its quiet splendour, a subtle promise of new beginnings. I settled into my familiar spot at the computer, the soft hum of the machine a comforting soundtrack to my early routine. Beside me, the steam from my morning cup of tea curled upwards in delicate tendrils, mingling with the crisp, cool air.

The tranquillity of the moment was almost sacred, a brief interlude before the chaos of the day unfolded. I inhaled deeply, savouring the earthy aroma of the tea, feeling its warmth seep into my hands and spread through my body. It was in these stolen moments of peace that I found my grounding.

But this serenity was merely the calm before the storm. I knew it was only a matter of time before the familiar, reassuring thud on my back – a signature of Jim's arrival – would jolt me from my reverie. That knowing slap, his unspoken signal, would mark the beginning of our next adventure into the digital abyss, a silent agreement that we were ready to dive back into the endless sea of code and creativity that awaited us.

The anticipation of that moment lingered in the air, thick and palpable. I braced myself for it, feeling the tension build as the seconds ticked by. Each passing heartbeat brought me closer to the inevitable, a crescendo of expectation that grew louder in the quiet morning. The slap would come, as it always did, with the force of a thousand possibilities. And when it did, I would be ready – ready to leap into the unknown, with Jim by my side, and face whatever challenges the day would bring.

The room was tense, thick with unspoken words and unresolved emotions. The air seemed to vibrate with the unyielding heat of confrontation. Without warning, the sharp, stinging sound of a slap pierced the silence. The impact reverberated through the room, echoing off the walls.

Jim's sudden arrival, snapped my head to the side from the force. A sharp intake of breath followed as I slowly turned back to face my assailant, a shadow of both shock and a smouldering fire in my eyes. The slap hung between us, a violent punctuation mark in the conversation we were about to have.

'Well, that was certainly unexpected', my voice was low, almost a growl, as I steadied myself. My gaze locked onto my counterpart with an intensity that could have melted steel. There was a heart-beat of silence before he responded, his tone now chillingly calm, a stark contrast to the volatile moment.

'I see you've been busy?' Jim's words sliced through the air, each syllable deliberate, measured. 'I did tell you not to delve into what I divulged to you.' His voice carried a warning, a reminder of the boundaries that had been breached. He took a step closer, eyes narrowing, every muscle in his body taut with suppressed emotion. 'So, now you've come across what you think is the story.' His lips curled into a bitter smile, one that didn't reach his eyes. 'But let me assure you, it's only the tip of the iceberg.'

The room seemed to grow colder, the weight of his words settling like a heavy cloak. Jim took a deep breath, as if gathering the threads of his composure. 'But let's leave that alone and move on to something brighter, shall we?' His voice lightened, but there was an edge to it, a dark undercurrent that suggested the brightness he referred to was anything but. He extended his hand, a gesture of formal greeting, as if to re-establish a fragile truce.

The formal handshake that followed was filled with unspoken tension, each squeeze a silent testament to the turbulent undercurrents between us. It was strange shaking hands with a person who has been dead for more than ninety years. I have shaken hands with a spiritual guide in a psychical circle, and I can tell you it's a very strange feeling indeed. The hand felt spongier than that of a real hand.

Jim's eyes never left me, a silent challenge issued with the contact. As we released the handshake, Jim's expression softened ever so slightly, but the intensity remained. The game had changed, and the pieces were now in motion. Whatever lay beneath the surface was bound to erupt, and both of us knew it.

The conversation had only just begun, and the slap was merely a prelude to the storm that was brewing. But for now, Jim seemed intent to explain some of the mysteries of his life in the astral plane.

'Let me unveil to you the splendour crafted by the architects of my realm. Imagine a cosmos where fourteen distinct planes of existence unfold – seven celestial planes above and seven subterranean realms below. Each plane is a masterpiece of cosmic design, woven together by the intricate dance of Energy, Frequency and Vibration. The Celestial Heights above us… the seven celestial planes shimmer with ethereal brilliance. These lofty realms are home to the most enlightened beings and grandest of creations:

1. The Luminous Spire: The first plane radiates pure light, a beacon visible across the cosmos. Here, light manifests in forms we can barely comprehend, each ray carrying whispers of ancient wisdom and the essence of pure creativity. This plane is a sanctuary for beings of light, who harness the vibrant energy to craft structures of crystalline beauty, forever shifting in hue and form.
2. The Symphony of the Spheres: Ascending higher, the second plane is a realm of pure sound. The air itself hums with the harmonic resonance of the universe. Majestic citadels made of resonant crystals dot the landscape, each vibrating in perfect symphony. Here, architects use sound to shape reality, creating edifices that sing with the harmonics of existence.
3. The Garden of the Gods: The third plane is a boundless expanse of lush greenery, where flora and fauna thrive in

perfect harmony. The landscape is sculpted by the flow of energy, forming gardens that bloom in response to the frequencies that pulse through them. Towers of living wood rise toward the heavens, their branches bearing fruits of knowledge and enlightenment.

4. The Forge of Stars: The fourth plane is a vast expanse of molten energy, where stars are born and forged. Here, architects harness the raw power of creation, crafting celestial bodies and intricate designs from the very fabric of the cosmos. It's a realm of endless possibility, where energy and matter converge to give birth to new worlds.

5. The Azure Citadel: The fifth plane is a serene realm of clear skies and tranquil waters. Floating islands adorned with opulent palaces drift effortlessly above vast oceans. The structures here are made of translucent materials, reflecting the plane's pristine nature and the delicate balance of frequencies that sustain it.

6. The Eternal Observatory: On the sixth plane, great observatories pierce the sky, gazing into the infinity of space. This is the realm of knowledge and insight, where scholars and architects delve into the mysteries of the universe. Towers of pure energy rise here, each a conduit for the frequencies that transmit the secrets of existence.

7. The Apex of Ascendance: The seventh and highest plane is a realm of pure consciousness. Here, form and structure dissolve into a sea of vibrant energy and thought. It's a place of ultimate enlightenment, where the architects channel the highest vibrations to create structures of pure thought, each a reflection of the infinite possibilities of the mind.

'The Subterranean Depths below us… the seven lower planes delve into the depths of existence, each with its own unique essence and character:

1. The Veil of Shadows: The first of the lower planes is a realm cloaked in perpetual twilight. Here, shadows dance with a life

of their own, and structures are crafted from the dark energy that permeates the realm. Architects weave these shadows into labyrinthine castles, where every corner holds secrets and the unknown lingers in the air.

2. The Abyssal Forge: Descend further to the second plane, a realm of raw, unbridled energy. It's a place where molten rock flows like rivers and the air crackles with the intensity of untamed forces. Architects here shape formidable fortresses from the very essence of the plane, their structures pulsating with the rhythms of the core energy.

3. The Echoing Caverns: The third plane is a vast expanse of caverns and tunnels, where every sound reverberates with profound depth. Architects carve out monumental halls and subterranean cities, where every whisper is amplified and resonates through the stone. Structures here are designed to harness and amplify the plane's resonant frequencies, creating spaces that seem to sing with the voice of the earth.

4. The Crystal Depths: On the fourth plane, glittering crystals of every hue form vast networks of natural structures. These crystals vibrate with the energies of the plane, casting dazzling light and shadows. Architects use these vibrant materials to craft magnificent cities that pulse with the harmonics of the subterranean frequencies.

5. The Infernal Citadel: The fifth plane is a realm of fire and brimstone, where infernal flames lick the sky. Structures here are forged from the heat and power of the plane, creating citadels that glow with an inner fire. Architects harness the inferno to shape fortresses of immense strength, each a testament to the raw power and intensity of the plane.

6. The Abyssal Maw: The sixth plane is a dark, tumultuous expanse where chaos reigns. Swirling vortices of energy and matter create a constantly shifting landscape. Architects here are masters of adapting to the ever-changing environment, crafting structures that flow and morph with the chaotic energies of the plane.

7. The Nether Nexus: The seventh and deepest plane is a realm of absolute stillness and void. Here, silence is the defining feature, and the absence of energy creates a space of profound emptiness. Architects in this plane create structures that embody the essence of the void, each a testament to the power of nothingness and the infinite potential it holds.

'Each plane, with its unique blend of Energy, Frequency and Vibration, contributes to the grand tapestry of our existence. Together, they form a universe of unparalleled complexity and beauty – a realm where the boundless creativity of the architects shapes the very fabric of reality.

'I know what you're thinking, Stephen. It all sounds very complicated, right? But let me share with you a revelation I encountered during one of my lessons in the hallowed halls of learning. Imagine a place – not bound by walls or time – where knowledge flows like an endless river and where each drop contains the essence of creation itself. This is not a place of forced attendance; here, the power of choice reigns supreme. We are beckoned, not commanded, by the allure of understanding. These halls, though not compulsory, draw us in with an irresistible promise – the deepening of our consciousness and the expansion of our awareness. In this sanctuary of wisdom, every soul is a seeker, driven by an innate curiosity to decode the mysteries of existence. Here, we do not merely learn; we evolve. We gather, not because we must, but because we are irresistibly drawn to the lectures that resonate with our deepest yearnings. It is within these lessons that we discover fragments of the cosmic puzzle that defines our place in the grand tapestry of creation.

'Consider this: each of us has an innate drive to understand the world around us, to seek out the truths that lie beyond the veil of our immediate perception. This drive propels us forward, guiding us to the knowledge that most closely aligns with our unique journey. In the halls of learning, this drive is nurtured and celebrated. We are free to follow the path that speaks to us most profoundly, to choose the lectures that ignite our passion and curiosity.

'These halls are not just a repository of facts and figures; they are a realm of infinite possibilities, where every question is an invitation to explore deeper, to think broader. They represent the pinnacle of what it means to be human – relentless pursuit of understanding, the courage to ask the unanswerable, and the humility to accept that every answer opens the door to new questions.

'When we attend these lectures, we do so not merely to gain knowledge, but to transform ourselves. Each lesson we absorb, each idea we contemplate, becomes a part of us, shaping our perspectives, our beliefs, and ultimately, our reality. This is the essence of learning: not just the acquisition of information, but the profound integration of wisdom into the fabric of our being.

'Stephen, the complexity that you perceive is but a reflection of the intricate beauty of the universe. It is through engaging with this complexity that we find clarity. The lectures in these halls may seem daunting at first, but they are meticulously crafted to guide us gently from the known into the unknown, from simplicity into the profound. In these sacred spaces, we are not passive recipients of knowledge; we are active participants in the dance of creation. We are given the freedom to explore, to question, to imagine. It is through this freedom that we discover our true potential, our capacity to contribute to the ever-unfolding story of existence.

'Therefore, Stephen, while the journey through these halls may appear complicated, it is also profoundly liberating. It invites us to step beyond the confines of our current understanding and to embrace the limitless expanse of possibility. Here, in the pursuit of wisdom, we find not only answers but also the courage to ask more meaningful questions. We find not just knowledge but also a deeper connection to the very essence of life.

'As we continue to navigate these halls, let us do so with a sense of wonder and gratitude. For in every lesson we encounter a glimpse of the divine, a spark of the infinite. And it is through this encounter that we come to understand that the true purpose of learning is not just to know, but to become – to become more aware, more compassionate, more alive.

'Death is often shrouded in mystery and fear, a looming enigma for those still bound to the earthly realm. But from where I now stand, on the other side of the veil, I can assure you that it is neither fearsome nor unknowable. In fact, it is a revelation – a journey into a realm so magnificent that words struggle to capture its essence. Imagine a life that transcends the mere physical; a life that pulses with a vibrancy and freedom that surpasses the most vivid of your earthly dreams. Here, we are not constrained by the limitations of the body or the burdens of material existence. We are free, truly free, in ways that the living can scarcely comprehend. In this world, every moment is infused with a profound sense of peace and purpose. The landscapes are more breathtaking than any earthly vista, alive with colours and sounds that resonate with the very essence of joy and tranquillity. The air is filled with a serene energy that envelops you, permeating every part of your being. Relationships here are deep and boundless, unencumbered by the misunderstandings and barriers that often plague connections on Earth. Communication transcends words; it is a pure and direct exchange of thoughts and feelings, a communion of spirits that fosters an unparalleled sense of unity and understanding.

'Time flows differently in this realm. It is fluid – a gentle current that carries us along in harmony with the universe's grand design. There is no rush, no urgency. Each experience is savoured, each moment cherished for its unique beauty and significance. This is a place of boundless opportunities for growth and exploration. We continue to learn, to evolve, and to fulfil our deepest desires and aspirations. Every soul is encouraged to follow their passions, to delve into the mysteries of existence, and to create and experience beyond the wildest imaginings of their earthly life.

'Death is not an end but a glorious beginning, a passage into a life that is richer, fuller and infinitely more liberating. It is a return to a home we have always known, a place where we are truly at peace, surrounded by love and light. It is, quite simply, wonderful. So, to those who still walk the earthly path, I say this: Fear not the unknown of death. Embrace the life you have, but know that what lies beyond is a realm of endless wonder and profound fulfilment. The freedom you seek in your world is but a shadow of the boundless liberation that awaits you here.

'Now, let me take you into the most intimate corners of my existence. Recently, I've had the immense fortune of meeting a captivating woman whose passions mirror my own. Our souls resonate with a shared love for the arts – whether it's the delicate grace of ballet that sweeps us off our feet, the profound verses of poetry that stir our deepest emotions, or the timeless narratives of plays that hold us in thrall. Beyond the grandeur of these cultural pursuits, we find solace and wonder in the enchanting parks that this spirit world offers.

'I cannot possibly convey the sheer brilliance of the colours that paint this paradise. Imagine flowers that shimmer in shades so vibrant, they seem to hum with life. The grass here is an entity unto itself – each blade a testament to the remarkable vitality of this realm. It glows with a green so pure, so full of light, that it feels almost unreal. As you walk, the ground beneath your feet yields softly, welcoming each step, only to spring back to its flawless form as if it had never been disturbed. It's as though the very essence of this world is alive, breathing, and in constant symphony with those who dwell here. The air is rich with fragrances that are both familiar and otherworldly, carrying whispers of stories untold. The trees, with their leaves fluttering in a gentle, perpetual breeze, seem to share their own silent wisdom. Each moment spent in these parks feels like a stolen piece of eternity, a reminder of the boundless beauty that pervades every corner of our existence.

'This connection I have formed is more than just a meeting of minds – it is a communion of spirits, a shared journey through a realm where every sight, every sound, every touch is an exquisite note in the symphony of the afterlife. Together, we wander through this paradise, two souls intertwined, discovering anew the wonders of a world where beauty knows no bounds, and life, in its purest form, continues to unfold in infinite splendour.

'Stephen, I love poetry. Only recently we went to a recital of one of Shakespeare's new poems. He has held on to his persona. Would you like to hear it?', Jim asked nervously.

'Yes, of course', I replied eagerly.

'Well, here goes', said Jim. 'It's called: *A Midsummer Night's Reverie*:

> *In leafy glade where moonbeams softly dance,*
> *The night doth whisper secrets to the earth,*
> *Fair sprites and dreams in silken robes advance,*
> *As time and wonder weave their subtle worth.*
>
> *The world doth sleep, but magic wakes to play,*
> *'Neath canopy of stars, a sparkling sky,*
> *Where shadows waltz and softly fade away,*
> *And lovers' sighs are lost on zephyrs' high.*
>
> *A silver brook through ancient wood doth flow,*
> *Its voice a serenade to those who hear,*
> *The murmured tales of love from long ago,*
> *Of passion, sorrow, joy and whispered fear.*
>
> *The velvet night, a cloak of deep embrace,*
> *Enfolds the world in tender, soothing arms,*
> *While fleeting visions softly kiss each face,*
> *And hearts are stilled by slumber's gentle charms.*
>
> *Oft have I wandered in this twilight hour,*
> *When dreams unfurl like petals in the night,*
> *And sought to pluck from time a single flower,*
> *To hold within my hand till morning's light.*
>
> *Yet fleeting is the hour of dream's domain,*
> *Where phantoms frolic on the edge of thought,*
> *And morn's first rays dispel the gentle rain*
> *Of visions, leaving memory distraught.*

The forest breathes a sigh as night grows deep,
Its boughs a cradle for the weary heart,
In whispered tones it lulls the soul to sleep,
Till daylight bids the drowsy world depart.

But lo, the moon doth rise on silver wings,
And casts a pallid glow on fields of green,
As fairies dance in dainty, twinkling rings,
Their laughter echoing through the serene.

The flowers bow their heads in silent prayer,
To moon and stars and all the heavens wide,
Their fragrance wafts upon the midnight air,
A perfume to the dreams where they abide.

The nightingale, with voice of liquid gold,
Doth sing a requiem to the darkened skies,
A song of tales forgotten, never told,
Of love and loss, and tender, longing cries.

Within this realm where shadows softly creep,
And dreams entwine with tendrils of the past,
I find a peace, profound and pure and deep,
That lingers long as night's embrace doth last.

For in the world of slumber, free from time,
Where thoughts and visions dance in wild array,
We find a truth transcendent and sublime,
A fleeting glimpse of dawn in night's array.

And as the stars their silent vigil keep,
And moonlight bathes the world in silver hue,
I drift within the arms of gentle sleep,
And whisper to the night my fond adieu.

Thus, let us cherish these ephemeral nights,
Where dreams and fancies bloom in twilight's care,
And hold within our hearts the fleeting sights,
Of reveries that fade with morning's glare.

> *For in the tender hush of midnight's grace,*
> *We find a solace that the day denies,*
> *A moment's peace, a touch, a soft embrace,*
> *Beneath the ever-watchful, starlit skies.'*

'How on earth were you able to remember all that?', I exclaimed, my voice tinged with awe and disbelief. My eyes widened, searching Jim's face for an explanation that could defy the boundaries of normal human capability.

Jim's gaze was distant, almost ethereal, as if he were peering into a realm far beyond our mundane reality. A slow, enigmatic smile spread across his face, giving him an almost otherworldly glow.

'It's not something you just stumble upon', he murmured, his voice soft yet resonant, like the whisper of ancient secrets carried on the wind. 'It's a skill honed over time, a gift cultivated through countless hours of introspection.'

He closed his eyes briefly, and I noticed a tranquil serenity enveloping him, as if he were attuned to a deeper, more profound frequency of existence. 'Through my meditation', he continued, his words flowing with a calm, rhythmic cadence, 'I've learned to expand the horizons of my mind. It's as if the fabric of my consciousness stretches beyond the confines of ordinary memory, tapping into a reservoir of knowledge that's vast and boundless.'

As he spoke, I felt a chill run down my spine, the weight of his revelation settling over me like a mystical fog. The room seemed to hum with an almost tangible energy, and for a moment, I wondered if Jim was more than just a man – if, perhaps, he held the secrets of the universe in the palm of his hand.

'Can you explain a little more about the above process?', I asked.

Jim's eyes gleamed with a fervour that seemed otherworldly. His voice, calm yet laced with an intense undercurrent of excitement, carried the weight of his discovery.

'Once we learn something, we can retain it', he said, his words hanging in the air like a prophecy. 'Not just in the fleeting, ephemeral way we're used to. No, it's much more profound than that.'

He paused, his gaze distant as if looking into a realm beyond the visible.

'When I close my eyes', he continued, his voice dropping to a whisper, 'I can recall anything that I have studied – every word, every image, as clear and vivid as the moment I first encountered it. It's like having a library within my mind, each book perfectly indexed, each fact ready to be summoned at will.'

He leaned forward, the intensity of his revelation drawing me closer, my breath held in anticipation.

'It's one of the many gifts that come to us when we are ready to embrace them', Jim said, his eyes now burning with a fierce light. 'These abilities, these extraordinary powers, lie dormant within us, waiting for the moment when we are prepared to unlock them. And when we do', he paused, his voice trembling with the sheer enormity of the thought, 'the world as we know it changes forever.'

The room fell into a profound silence. I was grappling with the implications of Jim's words. They were not merely skills or talents; they were keys to a new reality, a step beyond the ordinary, a leap into the boundless possibilities of the human spirit.

'In your world, Stephen, there exists a realm beyond the comprehension of most. It is a domain known intimately to advanced yogis and mystics, where the boundaries of time and space dissolve into a unified expanse of infinite knowledge. These adept practitioners possess the extraordinary ability to tap into this vast, cosmic repository of wisdom and insight. It is a celestial library, a compendium of all that ever was, is, and will be – an archive inscribed with the echoes of every thought, action and event that has ever transpired.

'In the terminology of your world, this boundless wellspring of knowledge is known as the Akashic Records. Envision it as an ethereal database, a metaphysical ledger where the entire history of the universe is meticulously recorded. It is said that those who can access these records can unlock the secrets of existence itself, gleaning profound truths that transcend the mundane reality of your everyday lives.

'Picture the Akashic Records as a shimmering, otherworldly library, where every soul's journey is catalogued in intricate detail. Here, past lives, future possibilities and the deepest truths of the cosmos are laid bare. The enlightened ones who can access this dimension do so through deep meditation and heightened spiritual attunement, transcending their mortal constraints to commune with the very essence of universal consciousness.

'Imagine, if you will, the wisdom contained in these records – how they hold the answers to the mysteries that have perplexed humanity for millennia. They are the ultimate source of knowledge, a divine treasure-trove that offers guidance and enlightenment to those who seek to understand the profound interconnectedness of all things. To tap into the Akashic Records is to glimpse the mind of the universe itself, to perceive the intricate patterns and infinite possibilities that weave the tapestry of existence.'

Jim's voice softened, yet his words carried a weight that hung heavy in the air. 'Stephen', he continued, his eyes reflecting both humility and determination, 'I have not yet ascended to that pinnacle of awareness, to the exalted state where one can effortlessly delve into the Akashic Records. It is a realm that still eludes my grasp – a level of enlightenment that I aspire to but have not yet attained.

'But do not mistake my current limitations for resignation or despair. I am resolute, steadfast in my commitment to the path laid before me by my teacher, Chan. He is more than a guide; he is a beacon in the vast darkness of my ignorance, a guardian of my spirit. Chan's wisdom, forged through lifetimes of spiritual practice, has illuminated the way for countless souls like mine. His teachings are not mere instructions but a lifeline, a meticulously crafted map that charts a course toward the very heart of universal truth.

'Every day, under Chan's vigilant guidance, I immerse myself in rigorous discipline. This discipline is not a burden but a sacred rite, a transformative process that reshapes my very being. Each meditation, each breath, each step is a deliberate movement toward awakening. I am like a sculptor chipping away at a block of stone, revealing the hidden statue within. Through my perseverance, the layers of my limited self are slowly being peeled away, uncovering the deeper, boundless consciousness that lies beneath.

'Chan's faith in me is unwavering. He sees within me the potential to access this cosmic reservoir of wisdom, to one day traverse the bridge to the Akashic Records. It is his belief in my capabilities that fuels my resolve, his vision of my future that propels me forward. Though I am not yet able to touch that sacred knowledge, I am on the path. Each day brings me closer, each moment of discipline, a step toward the extraordinary.

'So, I continue. Not because the journey is easy, but because it is essential. Not because I have already succeeded, but because the pursuit itself is a victory. And with Chan's wisdom guiding me, I know that no matter how distant the goal may seem, I will arrive. In time, I will reach that sublime state of awareness, where the Akashic Records open before me like a boundless sea of light, revealing the infinite expanse of the cosmos and the deepest truths of existence.'

Jim's words reverberated in the air, a testament to his unyielding spirit and his unwavering trust in his journey.

'Talking of Chan, can you tell us anything about this being?', I inquired, leaning forward with a mix of curiosity and unease. My companion hesitated, the weight of uncertainty settling heavily between us.

'This is quite awkward', he began, his voice tinged with an undercurrent of reverence and mystery. 'Truthfully, I do not know much about him, for Chan is an enigma even among the enlightened. What I do know is both fascinating and elusive. Chan is a being of profound wisdom, a guide of unparalleled knowledge who has resided in the spirit world for what seems like an eternity. His presence commands a silent respect among those who encounter him. His teachings are both gentle and formidable. He is the one who ushers souls like mine through the initial stages of our ethereal journey. The first, and perhaps most challenging lesson, is to grasp the full weight of our new reality – that we no longer dwell on the earthly plane, but have traversed into the realm of spirits. Chan helps us to shed the last vestiges of our mortal existence, guiding us to embrace the truth of our current state. His teachings are the foundation upon which our new understanding is built, preparing us for the vast and intricate journey that lies ahead in this otherworldly domain.'

As Jim spoke, I could almost feel the shadowy presence of Chan, a figure cloaked in the mysteries of the afterlife, his teachings stretching out like unseen tendrils, touching the very core of my being. The air around us seemed to thicken, the boundaries of the physical world blurring as I tried to comprehend the profound depths of this ancient, spectral guide.

'I have visited the sphere where Chan resides', Jim continued, 'which is a higher plane of existence. This realm is imbued with a luminosity and vibrational frequency that surpasses what I am accustomed to. It's a place where the energy is so pure and elevated that even a brief exposure can be overwhelming for souls from lower planes, like mine.

'When I say I visited, it's not as simple as just stepping into his world. The light and vibrational intensity in Chan's sphere are far beyond what my current level of spiritual evolution can handle comfortably. If I were to attempt entering without proper protection or adaptation, the sheer brilliance and high frequency could inundate my senses and potentially lead to a state of mental disorientation or distress. To mitigate this, I either need to be invited into Chan's sphere or wait until I evolve spiritually to a level where I can naturally resonate with its frequency. Being invited into such a sphere is an extraordinary privilege. It's akin to being given a precious gift because it involves the resident of the sphere – in this case, Chan – using their advanced abilities to create a protective cocoon around me. This protective cocoon acts like a filter, much like how sunglasses shield our eyes from the harshness of direct sunlight. Chan, through his advanced spiritual capabilities, can envelop me with his thoughts, effectively dampening the intense light and vibration. This allows me to experience the beauty and serenity of his sphere without being overwhelmed. Such an invitation not only demonstrates the generosity and compassion of the inviter but also provides a glimpse into a more evolved state of being, fostering profound gratitude and humility in the guest.

'This expansion highlights the challenges and nuances of traversing spiritual realms, emphasizing the need for protection when venturing into higher vibrational spheres. It illustrates the honour and transformative nature of being invited into such spaces by more advanced beings.'

'You spoke of frequencies: can you please explain a little more about this topic?', I asked curiously.

Jim's eyes flickered with a spark of intensity as he leaned forward, the weight of his words palpable. 'I'll do more than try', he declared with a resolute edge in his voice. 'You see, creation, as you understand it, is not merely a random act. It is a meticulous orchestration, an eternal symphony forged by the divine essence of the universe.'

He paused, letting the gravity of his statement settle in the air. 'This intricate tapestry of existence is woven from three fundamental threads of God's Will', he continued, his tone deepening with reverence. 'These threads are energy, frequencies and vibration.'

Jim's gaze seemed to pierce through the veil of ordinary understanding as he elaborated. 'Energy is the very lifeblood of creation, the boundless force that drives the cosmos. It is the pulse of stars, the flow of life, and the surge of every heartbeat. Without energy, there would be no light, no motion, no existence.'

Jim raised his hand, as if tracing the unseen waves around them. 'Frequencies', he said, his voice almost a whisper, 'are the divine rhythms that resonate through all things. They are the celestial melodies that bind the universe together, the harmonic whispers that govern the dance of atoms and galaxies alike. Every thought, every sound and every form is tuned to a frequency that shapes its reality.'

Finally, Jim's voice grew almost thunderous with passion. 'And then there is vibration – the heartbeat of the cosmos, the primal tremor that stirs the ether. It is the oscillation that brings form to the formless, the reverberation that breathes life into the void. Vibration is the silent roar of creation, the invisible hand that moulds the very fabric of reality.'

He paused, the air around him charged with a sense of profound mystery. 'These are not mere concepts', he concluded, his voice steady and filled with awe. 'They are the sacred forces through which the universe is sculpted, the divine will manifesting itself in every corner of existence. To understand them is to glimpse the very essence of creation itself.'

Jim leaned back, a quiet confidence in his eyes, the weight of his words lingering like an echo in the air. 'I'm tired', I whispered, my voice barely more than a breath.

Jim's eyes softened with understanding. 'That's okay, Stephen. We've done well today. Let's catch up tomorrow', he said, offering a gentle smile, leaving behind an eerie silence that filled the room and seeped into my bones. I rubbed my temples, trying to alleviate the dull throb that had settled behind my eyes. The long hours and relentless concentration had taken their toll, and now all I wanted was to escape into the comforting routine of the evening.

The promise of dinner beckoned. My stomach growled in anticipation of a hearty meal – roasted nut bake perhaps, with creamy mashed potatoes and steaming vegetables. The thought alone was almost enough to rouse my weary body. Almost. But what I craved even more was a glass of red wine, its rich aroma and velvety taste a balm for my frayed nerves.

Pushing myself up from the chair, I stretched, feeling the stiffness in my muscles. The sun had dipped below the horizon, casting the room in a twilight glow. I moved to the kitchen, the prospect of dinner urging me on. Later, I'd sink into the plush cushions of the couch, the wine glass cradled in my hand, and lose myself in the flickering light of a film. Something lighthearted, a distraction from the day's fatigue, before I surrendered to the pull of sleep.

For now, though, there was dinner to be savoured. I could almost taste the flavours mingling on my tongue, the warmth spreading through me. Yes, a good meal and a quiet evening were just what I needed. With a sigh, I set about preparing my modest feast, the kitchen filling with the comforting smells of home cooking. As my partner was away for the weekend, I had the honour of cooking for myself.

7
The Frequencies of Life

I rose with the first rays of dawn, the world still draped in a tranquil silence. The air was crisp as I made my way to the bathroom, the warmth of the shower washing away the remnants of sleep. Dressed and refreshed, I descended the worn, creaking stairs that whispered tales of countless mornings past.

In the kitchen, the faint light filtering through the curtains painted soft patterns on the floor. The kettle hummed eagerly, steam curling upwards as I prepared my morning elixir – a steaming cup of tea – its comforting aroma mingling with the promise of a new day. Beside it, the toaster chimed a cheerful tune as slices of bread transformed into golden perfection. A skillet sizzled with anticipation as I expertly whipped eggs into a creamy scramble, the buttery aroma dancing in the air.

Sated and invigorated by the simple pleasures of breakfast, I fortified myself for the challenges ahead. With resolve, I settled into my domain, the computer screen illuminating the room in a soft glow. And there, in the corner of my vision, was my steadfast companion and spectral confidant, Jim, whose presence lent an ethereal reassurance to the tasks that awaited.

Together, armed with determination and a more than a hint of otherworldly guidance, we embarked on another day of conquering challenges, navigating the digital realms where ideas flowed and creations took shape.

'Can you please explain more about energy, frequencies and vibration, and what Tesla revealed about his work when he was alive? I'm sure our readers would appreciate your input, Jim', I inquired, leaning forward with eager anticipation.

'Really? Well, if you insist', Jim chuckled softly, a mischievous twinkle igniting his eyes like embers in the dark. His voice, usually soft and spectral, now resonated with a lively cadence that drew me in just as a spellbinding tale.

'You see', he began, his words weaving a tapestry of cosmic mysteries, 'energy, frequencies, and vibrations – they are the very essence of our existence, intertwined in the fabric of the universe itself. Tesla, ah, now there was a mind attuned to the symphony of creation.' Jim paused momentarily, as if relishing a memory carried across realms.

'I've had the privilege', he continued, his voice carrying the weight of wisdom beyond his ethereal form, 'to attend one of his lectures here. His insights into the nature of reality, the dance of electrons and the unseen forces that bind us, they resonate deeply with my interests.' A faint smile played on his lips, hinting at secrets shared between dimensions. 'As I've delved deeper into such matters', Jim mused, his presence shimmering with a newfound vibrancy, 'I've come to appreciate the intricate harmony that governs all. Tesla was on to something profound – a symphony of vibrations orchestrating the cosmos, where every note, every frequency, plays its part in the grand design.'

His words lingered, echoing in the space between us, infusing the air with a sense of wonder and reverence for the mysteries that transcended mortal understanding. And in that moment, as I absorbed Jim's spectral wisdom, I couldn't help but marvel at the profound connection between past brilliance and present curiosity, bridged by a ghostly friend who had journeyed through time and thought to share his fascination with the cosmic dance of energy and vibration.

Jim continued his narrative and his admiration for this man. 'Nikola Tesla is often quoted for his fascination with the numbers 3, 6 and 9, and their significance in the universe. Although there is no concrete evidence in your world as yet that Tesla explicitly linked these numbers to the process of creation, his views and the interpretations around these numbers suggest a deeper philosophical or mystical significance. Tesla reportedly said: "If you only knew the magnificence of 3, 6 and 9, then you would have the key to the universe." This statement reflects his belief that these numbers have a profound significance, potentially offering insights into the workings of the universe. Let's explore possible interpretations:

1. Numerical patterns and harmonics; numerology: In numerology, the numbers 3, 6 and 9 are considered part of a unique group of "root" numbers with specific characteristics. Each number symbolizes different aspects: creativity (3), harmony (6) and universal understanding or completion (9).
2. Harmonics and frequencies: Tesla was deeply interested in frequencies and vibrations. The numbers 3, 6 and 9 are significant in the study of harmonics and could be seen as fundamental to the structure of sound and energy in the universe.
3. Vortex mathematics: This is a theory developed by Marko Rodin, who claims that 3, 6 and 9 form a pattern that underlies the universe's structure. According to Rodin, these numbers can represent a "flux field" and are key to understanding the energy dynamics of the universe. In vortex math, 3, 6 and 9 are seen as a central axis around which the other numbers rotate, creating a blueprint for energy flow and possibly for matter and creation itself.
4. Symbolism and geometry; sacred geometry: These numbers appear in various forms of sacred geometry. For example, the *vesica piscis*, which is formed by two intersecting circles, and other geometric shapes like the enneagram and flower of life, often highlight patterns involving 3, 6 and 9.

'Are you taking all this down, Stephen?'

'Yes, I'm typing it all down. If there are any mistakes, I'll ask you about them when I edit the manuscript.'

'Okay, then I'll continue. Now, where was I? Right...!

5. Tetrahedral and triangular relationships: The number 3 is the first prime number that forms a shape (triangle), which is the

basis for much of geometry. The combination of these numbers can be seen in structures like the tetrahedron, which is a building block in both molecular structures and cosmic formations.
6. Cyclic nature and repetition; repetition and patterns: In various natural phenomena, patterns based on the number 3, such as triplets, triangles and other threefold symmetries, are recurrent. The numbers 3, 6 and 9 are multiples of each other and could represent cycles or repetitions in nature.
7. Philosophical and esoteric beliefs: Some philosophies and esoteric teachings suggest that these numbers represent stages of creation and evolution. For example, the triad of birth, life and death or the three phases of creation, sustenance and destruction. In relation to creation: When considering creation, the numbers 3, 6 and 9 could be seen as representing different aspects or stages of the creative process:
8. *3*: The trinity of creation; beginning: The number 3 often symbolizes the initial creative impulse or triad. In many cultures, trinity structures (such as the Christian Holy Trinity or the Hindu Trimurti) represent the foundational aspects of creation, sustenance and destruction.
9. Simplicity and stability: A triangle, the simplest form that still encloses a space, suggests a fundamental stability in the universe.
10. *6*: The Process of manifestation, harmony and balance: The number 6 is associated with harmony and nurturing. It can represent the process of creation moving towards balance and fullness. Six-dimensional space: In physics, six dimensions can be seen in certain models of the universe where additional dimensions are compactified.
11. *9*: The completion or full cycle; fulfilment: The number 9 often symbolizes completion and the highest level of vibration or energy. It can be seen as the culmination of the creative process, where all energies and potentials converge. Universal

energy: In numerology, 9 represents universal love, eternity and the end of a cycle, indicating the point where creation is fully realized and possibly ready to begin anew.

'Tesla's reference to 3, 6 and 9 can be interpreted as a nod to these numbers' deep-seated connections to the structure and dynamics of the universe. Whether through numerology, sacred geometry, vortex mathematics or symbolic significance, these numbers resonate with the principles of creation, balance and completion. Understanding their relationship can offer insights into the fundamental patterns that govern the cosmos.'

'Good Lord, Jim', I exclaimed, my hands trembling uncontrollably as my fingers threatened to lock into a spasm. 'That was an astounding revelation!'

'Yes, Stephen', Jim replied gravely, his voice tinged with a mix of awe and apprehension. 'But what I've told you is only part of the truth. Nikola Tesla was not just a brilliant inventor; he was a visionary who saw the future with a clarity that few could comprehend. He once claimed to have discovered a method that could revolutionize our entire existence for the better. Tesla's dream was to harness and provide free, unlimited energy to every corner of the globe, to liberate humanity from the shackles of energy dependency. He envisioned a world where power lines would become obsolete, and every household could access the boundless energy of the universe.

'However, his grand vision was met with fierce resistance. J.P. Morgan, the powerful banker who initially funded Tesla's ventures, was captivated by Tesla's genius and the prospect of great profit. But when Tesla proposed the radical idea of distributing electricity freely to everyone, Morgan recoiled. The thought of free energy was a direct threat to the economic and industrial empires built on the control and sale of energy. Morgan, realizing that such a world would undermine his financial interests, swiftly turned against Tesla. Funding dried up, and Tesla's ambitious plans were buried under a mountain of skepticism and corporate greed. Yet, this was only the beginning of the mysteries surrounding Tesla. He claimed to have invented a weapon of such immense power that it could lay waste to armies and entire cities. This so-called "death ray" was rumoured to be capable of unleashing devastation on a scale never before seen. Whether this device was real or merely a fragment of Tesla's fevered imagination remains a topic of debate, but the fear it instiled was enough to mark him as a dangerous man in the eyes of many.

'When Tesla died in utter poverty in 1943, alone and forsaken, the U.S. government seized his papers, notes and drawings. Officially, these documents vanished into the labyrinth of bureaucratic archives. But whispers persisted that some of his most groundbreaking and controversial work had simply disappeared. Despite his physical demise, Tesla's genius lived on. He had a photographic memory, an unparalleled ability to recall and reconstruct his thoughts and inventions. This unique gift, coupled with his assertion during one of his last public lectures that he had connected to the divine records of creation, suggested that his intellectual legacy was far from extinguished.

'It's said that Tesla still influences the realm of science and technology from beyond the grave. Those who attended his final lecture reported that he spoke of tapping into the universal consciousness, a cosmic repository of knowledge. Even now, many believe that Tesla's spirit whispers to the minds of modern scientists and engineers, guiding them as they unravel the mysteries of the universe. He may no longer walk among you, but his influence continues to inspire and propel humanity towards a future he foresaw with unparalleled clarity.'

Jim paused, letting the weight of his words settle. 'Stephen, Tesla was more than a man; he was a beacon of possibilities. And, even now, his legacy flickers in the hearts of those who dare to dream as he did.'

I was utterly spellbound by his extraordinary ability to summon, without a single note, a lecture of such extensive length and depth. It was a masterclass.

'Though the concept of time in my realm', Jim began, 'diverges sharply from your earthly understanding. There, the passage of moments is but an illusion, for in my world night does not descend. Instead, we are perpetually bathed in an ethereal light that emanates from the higher inner sphere, a luminescence that is both warm and invigorating. This constant glow is not just a physical phenomenon; it is a manifestation of the profound knowledge and wisdom that permeates our existence.'

Every word of Jim's discourse seemed to be infused with this radiant brilliance, resonating with the timeless and boundless nature of our reality.

'Well, Jim, I have to admit', I began, leaning back in my chair with a look of genuine astonishment, 'you've truly opened my eyes this morning. I thought I had a grasp on things, but you've taken me on a deep dive into a topic I scarcely understood. Your insights have been nothing short of enlightening.'

Jim smiled, a glint of pride in his eyes. 'I'm glad to hear that', he said. 'There's always more to learn and understand.'

I nodded, feeling a surge of curiosity. 'Absolutely. But now', I continued, with a playful yet serious tone, 'I'm eager to pick your brain on another topic that's been swirling around in the public discourse.' Jim's expression shifted to one of keen interest. 'By all means', he replied, gesturing for me to continue. 'What's on your mind?'

I took a breath, choosing my words carefully. 'There's been a lot of buzz lately about climate change. People everywhere are talking about it – the science, the politics, the impact on our daily lives. It feels like a puzzle with pieces scattered across the globe. Could you help me piece it together?'

'Certainly! But I must admit, the intricacies of climate control in your world elude me. Allow me a moment to find someone more versed in this matter from my side of life.' Jim's voice carried a note of curiosity, tinged with the promise of uncovering a solution.

As Jim retreated to investigate, I felt a wave of relief wash over me. This would give me a much-needed break. The tension in my shoulders eased slightly at the thought. I had two pressing needs: a steaming cup of tea to soothe my nerves and the urgent call of nature that could no longer be ignored.

'Stephen', Jim's voice rang out again, now filled with determination. 'Let's take a brief intermission while I delve into finding the right expert. I'll be back before you know it.' I nodded, grateful for the reprieve. Jim's initiative gave me hope, but more importantly, it gave me time to address my own immediate needs. I hurried to the kitchen, the prospect of a hot, calming brew quickening my steps. The kettle's hiss was like a symphony promising relief. Yet even as I prepared my tea, my mind wandered back to our discussion. The concept of climate control had always fascinated me, and the potential of unlocking its secrets now seemed tantalizingly close. But before I could dive back into the depths of inquiry, there was another call I could no longer ignore – the bathroom beckoned with an insistence that could not be postponed.

With my tea in hand and the door to the WC firmly closed behind me, I allowed myself a brief moment of respite. Jim's promise of assistance from his side of life lingered in my mind, a beacon of hope amidst the mysteries we sought to unravel.

As I settled into my chair, the gentle clinking of my teacup resonated through the room, a sound almost drowned by the muted hum of the computer. Steam swirled in whimsical patterns above the delicate china, mingling with the earthy aroma of freshly brewed tea. The biscuits lay on a plate beside me, their golden edges promising a momentary escape into crisp sweetness. Just as I prepared to indulge in this small pleasure, the tranquil scene was abruptly shattered. Jim burst onto the scene, a flurry of motion that disrupted the stillness. He was not alone. Beside him stood an imposing and enigmatic figure whose presence commanded immediate attention.

Jim, usually composed and deliberate, appeared uncharacteristically agitated. With a glance that darted between me and our mysterious visitor, he cleared his throat, attempting to regain his usual authoritative demeanour.

'Allow me to introduce our guest', he announced, his voice strained with a mix of urgency and reverence. 'This is F.K.S.' The initials hung in the air, laden with significance. They seemed to carry a weight far beyond their simple alphabetical representation. I scrutinized the man standing before me, trying to decipher the mystery cloaked in those three letters.

F.K.S. was an enigma wrapped in a crisp, tailored suit. His eyes, sharp and observant, missed nothing. They flicked over my desk, taking in the teacup, the biscuits, and finally meeting my own gaze with an intensity that sent a shiver down my spine. There was something about him – an aura of authority and an undercurrent of danger – that made my fingers tremble ever so slightly as they gripped the armrests of my chair.

As Jim stepped aside, allowing F.K.S. to advance, I couldn't shake the feeling that my quiet moment with tea and biscuits had been the calm before a brewing storm. F.K.S. suddenly leaned forward, and his eyes glinted with a peculiar intensity. He began speaking in an accent that wavered between the lilt of a seasoned sea captain and the deliberate enunciation of an erudite professor. It was an accent steeped in mystery, one that evoked the windswept coasts of distant lands and the hallowed halls of ancient academies.

'Good day, young man', he declared, his voice echoing with a gravitas that commanded my attention. 'I understand you seek enlightenment on the rudiments of climate change?' His words hung in the air, imbued with a weight that made the subject seem both immensely significant and profoundly complex. My heart raced, and I swallowed hard, my throat suddenly dry.

'Yes, please', I replied, my voice a mere whisper, betraying the nervous flutter in my chest. I felt like an apprentice standing before a grand master, eager yet apprehensive about the knowledge that was to come. F.K.S. smiled, a knowing glimmer in his eyes, as if he could see the swirling maelstrom of thoughts within me.

'Well then', he said, his tone softening yet maintaining its authoritative edge, 'I shall endeavour to illuminate the intricate dance of nature and humanity that is climate change. I will strive to distil the essence of what occupies the minds of scientists today into something clear and comprehensible for you.'

He paused, his gaze drifting momentarily to the window where the light of the setting sun cast a golden hue over the room, as if gathering the elements of the story he was about to weave. I sat transfixed, ready to embark on this journey of understanding, guided by his enigmatic presence.

He began by saying, 'The conversation around climate change is vast and multifaceted, intersecting science, politics and everyday life. Let's delve into each of these components to understand them more clearly. *Greenhouse gases*: climate change primarily refers to the long-term changes in temperature and weather patterns on Earth. This is largely driven by the increase in greenhouse gases (GHGs) such as carbon dioxide (CO_2), methane (CH_2) and nitrous oxide (N_2O). These gases trap heat in the atmosphere, creating a 'greenhouse effect' that warms the planet.

'Earth's climate has changed throughout history due to natural causes like volcanic eruptions and variations in solar radiation. However, since the Industrial Revolution (~1750), human activities have accelerated these changes. Global temperatures have risen approximately 1.1°C above pre-industrial levels, with significant increases in recent decades. *Glacial melt and sea-level rise*: polar ice caps and glaciers are melting at unprecedented rates, contributing to rising sea levels. This not only threatens coastal communities but also affects global weather patterns.

'There's an increase in the frequency and severity of extreme weather events such as hurricanes, droughts and wildfires in your world. Scientists on earth use complex models to predict future climate scenarios based on different levels of GHG emissions. These models suggest significant warming and climatic changes if current trends continue. Certain thresholds, or tipping points, could lead to irreversible changes in the climate system, such as the collapse of the Greenland ice sheet or major shifts in ocean currents.

'*The Paris Agreement*: adopted in 2015, this international treaty aims to limit global warming to well below 2°C, preferably to 1.5°C, compared to pre-industrial levels. It involves commitments from nearly all countries to reduce their emissions. *Kyoto Protocol*: an earlier agreement that set binding emission reduction targets for developed countries, which expired in 2020. Many countries are implementing carbon pricing mechanisms, such as carbon taxes or cap-and-trade systems, to incentivize reductions in GHG emissions. Governments are promoting renewable energy sources (solar, wind, hydro) through subsidies and investment in technology to reduce dependence on fossil fuels.

'Transitioning to a low-carbon economy can be challenging for industries and economies reliant on fossil fuels. This creates a tension between economic growth and environmental sustainability. Climate change disproportionately affects poorer nations and communities, raising issues of climate justice. There's an ongoing debate about the responsibilities of developed vs. developing countries in addressing climate change. Increased air pollution from burning fossil fuels can lead to respiratory and cardiovascular diseases. Rising temperatures increase the risk of heat-related illnesses and deaths, particularly among vulnerable populations like the elderly and those with pre-existing conditions.

'Now we come to *changing weather patterns*, which can affect crop yields, leading to food shortages and increased prices. Glacial melt and changing precipitation patterns can disrupt water supplies, affecting agriculture, drinking water and sanitation. Individuals and communities are adapting by conserving energy, reducing waste, and making sustainable choices in food, travel and consumption. Local initiatives are strengthening community resilience to climate impacts through improved infrastructure, disaster preparedness and sustainable practices. Shifting to renewable energy, enhancing energy efficiency and adopting cleaner technologies are key strategies for reducing emissions. Techniques such as reforestation, soil management, and carbon capture and storage (CCS) help remove CO_2 from the atmosphere. Building flood defences, improving water management systems and designing heat-resilient buildings help communities adapt to climate impacts. Protecting and restoring natural ecosystems enhances their resilience to climate changes and supports biodiversity. Individuals can reduce their carbon footprint through lifestyle changes like using public transportation, reducing meat consumption and supporting sustainable products. Participating in climate activism, supporting policies for sustainability and educating others are powerful ways to drive collective action.

'Understanding climate change involves piecing together these diverse elements – from the science explaining why and how your planet is changing, to the political frameworks guiding your response, to the tangible impacts on your daily lives and the actions you can take. Addressing climate change requires a multifaceted approach, involving global cooperation, innovative solutions and proactive steps from every level of society.

'Well', he clarified, 'this is the path your globalists are upon right now. But let me reveal a truth so staggering it will shatter the very foundations of your understanding. The worst is yet to come, and it's a fate no one will be able to forestall. You believe the fight against climate change is simply a battle against the relentless consumption of fossil fuels. Yet that is but a surface concern, a mere distraction from the true peril lurking beneath your feet. The most catastrophic threat lies not in the carbon-laden skies or the polluted oceans, but in the dark, unfathomable depths of the Earth itself.

'The very core of your planet is slowing its rotation. This primal force, the throbbing heart of your world, is decelerating, sending ripples of chaos through the Earth's delicate balance. Imagine it: the tectonic plates slipping, the magnetic fields faltering, the axis of the Earth wobbling in an unpredictable dance. These are not just speculations of a fevered mind – they are the impending harbingers of a new era of climate upheaval. The danger here is to the electromagnetic field which surrounds your earth. It is this profound disturbance that will unleash a torrent of climatic cataclysms far beyond your current nightmares. Unchecked by any human endeavour, this deep Earth phenomenon will ravage ecosystems, rewrite weather patterns and plunge humanity into a relentless struggle for survival.

'Do you feel the gravity of this revelation? Can you comprehend the enormity of the storm on the horizon? I think I've unveiled enough for your readers to contemplate – a glimpse into a future where the very ground beneath your feet is the source of your greatest woes.'

With a sincere and profound appreciation that swelled within me, I expressed my heartfelt thanks to him for his illuminating insights. His wisdom pierced through the fog of confusion surrounding one of the most pressing issues of our time – an issue that occupies the thoughts and fears of countless individuals who are deeply concerned about the future of our planet and the unfolding climate crisis. His words resonated deeply, offering clarity and hope in a world grappling with the shadow of environmental uncertainty. With that, he bid us farewell and departed, leaving Jim and me to finish the day together.

'What did you think of him?', Jim asked. I began slowly, my mind reeling with thoughts. 'I'm at a loss for words right now', I replied, my curiosity piqued. I leaned back, my expression thoughtful. 'I must admit, he left quite an impression. But tell me, why do you think he refused to divulge his name?', I inquired, though a sinking feeling already hinted at the answer.

'I believe', Jim responded, his voice tinged with a hint of solemnity, 'that he once held great prominence in your world. Here, names are merely waypoints, devoid of the weight they carry elsewhere.' His words hung in the air, resonating with a profound truth that both intrigued and unsettled me.

'Time to stop', I declared firmly, my voice tinged with exhaustion. 'I need my rest. It's all well and good for you, Jim, but I still need to eat, drink, and, of course, to sleep!'

As the weight of my words settled in the air, Jim finally took the hint. With a courteous nod and a brief 'Good evening', he quietly made his exit, leaving me alone in the dwindling twilight.

Food and a glass of wine beckoned urgently, from the depths of my hunger and weariness. With my partner still absent, the solitude of the kitchen awaited my touch. I ventured into its familiar confines, seeking solace in the ritual of preparing a meal. The clatter of pots and pans echoed my thoughts, a symphony of hunger and exhaustion orchestrating my movements.

In the sanctuary of the kitchen, I meticulously crafted a meal, drawing comfort from the sizzle of ingredients meeting the pan, the aromatic dance of spices in the air. The rhythmic pour of red wine into a waiting glass marked a moment of respite, a pause in the whirlwind of demands and responsibilities. As I raised the glass to my lips, the ruby elixir offered not just refreshment, but a fleeting escape from the day's trials. Each sip spoke of evenings past, shared moments now suspended in memory. The warmth of the wine mirrored the fire within, kindling a sense of peace amidst the storm.

In that kitchen, amidst the clink of cutlery and the soft glow of evening light, I found a sanctuary. Here, nourishment transcended mere sustenance, becoming a communion of body and soul, a sanctuary in the stillness of an unfinished day.

8

Relationships

The early morning beckoned with a serene beauty that enveloped everything in its gentle embrace. The air was crisp and laden with the delicate scent of dew-kissed grass and blossoming flowers. As the first light timidly peeked over the horizon, casting a golden glow upon the world, I found myself drawn to the quietude that only dawn could offer.

Being an early riser was more than a habit – it was a sacred ritual. It allowed me to savour the precious moments when the world was still hushed, and possibilities stretched out before me like an endless road. In those tranquil hours, thoughts wandered freely, dreams took flight, and the day's potential seemed boundless.

The early morning was not merely a time of day; it was a sanctuary where I could gather my thoughts, find solace in the gentle rhythm of awakening nature, and prepare myself for the challenges and joys that lay ahead. It was a time when the essence of life itself felt palpable, urging me to seize the day with a heart full of gratitude and anticipation.

My morning ritual of tea and toast had come to an end, the comforting warmth of the steaming brew soothing my senses. With a fresh cup of tea in hand, I settled down at my desk, ensuring to place the tea well away from my computer. I had learned the hard way, for on occasions when Jim arrived, his energetic greetings had nearly sent my tea flying, as if he had a knack for knocking it right out of my grasp.

'Jim's late', I thought – a notion that seemed almost inconceivable. In the realm where he now resided, how did they even measure time? Was there a concept of night and day in the spirit world? I pondered these mysteries as I delved deeper into the manuscript before me, eagerly anticipating his arrival.

Moments stretched into minutes, each second laden with expectation until, abruptly, the air around me seemed to shimmer with his unmistakable presence. The familiar cadence of his voice, so reassuring yet tinged with an otherworldly quality, broke through the stillness. It was as if the very atmosphere responded to his arrival, imbuing the room with a sense of anticipation and warmth that only his presence could bring.

'Sorry I was a bit hung up', he announced cheerfully, his eyes sparkling with an undeniable mischief that set my curiosity on edge. It was clear he had been involved in something amusing or intriguing, and I couldn't resist probing further. 'What are you laughing about?' I inquired bluntly, my tone tinged with both amusement and a touch of suspicion, eager to unravel the mystery behind his infectious smile.

'Oh, I've just come from a concert with my new girlfriend', he replied.

'So you have relationships over there in the spirit world then?', I enquired.

'In my world, Stephen, relationships are vastly different from those on Earth. Here, we unite through a profound mental connection, transcending mere physical or sexual attraction. It's a bond woven from the threads of intellect, emotion and shared understanding, where the meeting of minds sparks a symphony of souls. Our connection deepens through the resonance of ideas and the harmony of thoughts, creating a tapestry of intimacy that goes beyond the limitations of the flesh. It's a union where the meeting of minds ignites a cosmic dance of hearts, weaving together a story of connection that defies earthly conventions.

'In the spiritual realm, love and sexuality intertwine in a tapestry woven with ethereal threads, transcending the physical manifestations of desire. Here, love is a radiant beacon that illuminates the soul, nurturing a profound sense of unity and belonging. It's a love that surpasses the limitations of earthly perceptions, embracing a deeper understanding of self and other. Sexuality, in this realm, becomes a sacred dance of energies, where intimacy is not merely physical but a merging of essences. It's an expression of spiritual connection, where souls intertwine in a harmonious exchange of energy and emotion. This union transcends the confines of gender or form, resonating with the pure essence of love and compassion.

'In the spiritual world, relationships are rooted in mutual respect, trust and a shared journey of spiritual growth. Partnerships are built on the foundation of deep understanding and acceptance, where each soul supports the other's evolution towards higher consciousness. Here, love is expansive and inclusive, embracing the diversity of experiences and expressions. It's a celebration of unity in diversity, where each soul contributes to the collective tapestry of love and spirituality. It's a realm where the beauty of love radiates through every interaction, transcending time and space to weave a timeless saga of interconnected souls on a journey of profound love and spiritual evolution.'

'Well, that's interesting', I remarked, my eyebrows arching in surprise. I paused for a moment, letting the statement sink in before continuing with a touch of disbelief, 'So, let me get this straight – there's strictly no allowance for any kind of sexual expression in your world?'

'That's exactly what I just said, didn't I!' Jim's initial reaction to my question was transparently tense, his brows furrowing with a hint of irritation. However, as our conversation unfolded, he gradually softened, his demeanour transforming from being defensive to contemplative.

Jim continued: 'Sexuality in your world is an all-encompassing pursuit, a deeply ingrained facet of human nature that transcends mere physicality. It is an intricate tapestry woven from desire, intimacy and connection – a labyrinth of emotions and experiences that shape our identities and relationships. At its core, sexuality is a profound exploration of pleasure and fulfilment, a quest for understanding and self-discovery that navigates the complexities of human desire.

'In every corner of our existence, from the whispers of intimate moments to the bold declarations of love, sexuality weaves its threads, influencing our perceptions, motivations, and interactions. It is both a reflection of our individuality and a bridge between souls, a universal language spoken through touch, gaze and shared vulnerability.'

Jim's initial unease melted away as he began to embrace the depth and nuance of our discussion. He acknowledged the multifaceted nature of sexuality, recognizing its power to both exhilarate and challenge our perceptions. Our dialogue became a journey of exploration, delving into the nuances of desire and the intricacies of human connection, where each revelation uncovered new layers of understanding and empathy. Ultimately, our exchange transcended mere words, becoming a testament to the profound impact of sexuality on our lives – a dynamic force that shapes our experiences, relationships and the very essence of who we are.

'Well, I've found myself utterly captivated by a soul so profoundly beautiful, a rare gem in the tapestry of life', Jim mused with an air of deep introspection. 'She's not just someone I admire; she's a muse whose presence has woven magic into the fabric of my time here.' His voice, normally steady, now carried a lyrical cadence as he continued: 'In her, I've discovered a reservoir of wisdom that transcends the mundane, a fountain of mental exhilaration that quenches the thirst of my restless mind. Each conversation with her is like embarking on an epic voyage across uncharted seas, where every word she utters is a constellation, guiding me through the cosmos of thoughts and emotions.'

Jim's eyes lit up with a fervour reserved for those who have found something truly extraordinary. 'Her laughter dances like sunlight on water, and her words are like gentle breezes that stir the depths of my soul. She has shown me the beauty in vulnerability and the strength in embracing the unknown. In her presence, Stephen, I feel as though I've uncovered a treasure-trove of truths that resonate deep within.'

He paused, as if savouring the memory of moments spent in her company. 'To know her is to witness the world through a kaleidoscope of colours, each hue more vibrant than the last. She has opened my eyes to the poetry of existence, where every moment becomes a verse in the symphony of life.' Jim's expression softened, a tender smile playing on his lips. 'She has taught me that true beauty lies not in perfection, but in the courage to be authentic. In her, I've found a kindred spirit, a companion on this journey of self-discovery and growth. She is the muse who inspires my heart to sing and my mind to soar.'

His voice, now a whisper tinged with reverence, conveyed the depth of his emotions. 'In her presence, I am reminded that life is a tapestry woven from moments of connection and understanding. She is my muse, my confidante and my guide through the labyrinth of existence.' As he spoke, it was evident that Jim had found more than admiration; he had found a soulmate whose presence illuminated his world with boundless wonder and whimsy – a beacon in the journey of life's unfolding mysteries.

'Okay Jim, I'm starting to piece it together now. You've fallen hard, haven't you, mate?'

'Well, if I'm being completely honest, yes, I think I have.'

'Wow, tell me everything! What was the concert like? Who stole the spotlight?'

'Oh, it was absolutely incredible! Picture this: opera arias echoing through the air, sung by some truly amazing voices. My new girlfriend is a huge opera fan, and she convinced me to join her at this outdoor concert in the park. Stephen, let me tell you, the setting couldn't have been more perfect. The gardens were stunning, bathed in the soft glow of our light, and then there was the music…!

'The voices were like nothing I've ever heard before. Each aria filled the air with emotion, passion and skill. But you know who stole the spotlight? There was this one soprano, her voice soared effortlessly through the air, commanding attention with every note. She had the entire audience spellbound, myself included. It was mesmerizing, Stephen, simply mesmerizing. And the atmosphere! It was like being transported to another world, where every worry melted away in the beauty of the moment. The combination of the music, the setting, and the company made it an unforgettable experience. I've never appreciated opera like I did that evening. I can't wait to go again. It was truly magical, Stephen, absolutely magical.'

'How did you meet your new girlfriend?', I inquired, my curiosity piqued.

'Well, it's a bit of a story that one', he began, a wistful smile playing on his lips. 'You see, it was Chan who pushed me to finally step out of my comfort zone. He kept saying that I needed to find a way to express myself, and he wouldn't stop talking about this art class he had discovered.' Jim paused, his eyes distant, as if replaying the scene in his mind. 'I've always had a soft spot for art. There's something about the way colours blend, the way a single stroke can change everything. So I thought, why not? I signed up, more out of curiosity than anything else.'

He leaned forward, his voice lowering as if sharing a secret. 'That first day, I was nervous as hell. But as soon as I walked into that studio, I felt a strange sense of calm wash over me. The room was filled with the smell of paint and the quiet murmur of people lost in their own worlds. I found an empty seat and settled in, hoping to disappear into the background.' Jim's eyes lit up as he continued. 'But then, she walked in. Anna. She had this air about her, like she belonged in that world, like she was part of the canvas itself. She glanced around the room and, as if by fate, chose the seat right next to mine.'

He chuckled softly, shaking his head. 'At first, we didn't say much. Just polite nods and awkward smiles. But then, as the class went on, we started to chat. It was nothing serious, just small talk about the painting we were working on. But there was something in her voice, something in the way she spoke about art, that drew me in.'

He paused, his expression growing more animated. 'Before I knew it, we were talking about everything – our favourite artists, our dreams, our fears. It was like we had known each other forever. We discovered we had so much in common, from our love of Impressionism to our shared obsession with obscure documentaries.' He leaned back, a satisfied look on his face. 'By the end of that class, I knew I had to see her again. And the rest, as they say, is history. We've been inseparable ever since.'

As he finished, he glanced at me, his eyes shining with the kind of joy that only comes from finding something truly special. 'So, yeah, that's how I met Anna. Thanks to a little push from Chan and a serendipitous seat in an art class.'

'What has she said about your work on the lower astral plane?', I enquired.

'Well, revealing the true nature of my duties to her felt like treading on forbidden ground. Everyone was acutely aware of the relentless, harrowing battles raging in the lower astral realms, a war that whispered through the very fabric of our existence. The darkness of those conflicts lingered in the air, a silent reminder of the perilous tasks we undertook daily.

'Our superiors had issued strict orders: our work was to remain shrouded in secrecy, a veil that must not be lifted, not even for those closest to us. The weight of that command bore down on me, pressing my lips tightly shut each time she asked. But she was persistent – her curiosity growing with each passing day. Her eyes would lock on to mine, searching for cracks in the façade I maintained. "What is it that you do?", she would ask, her voice a mix of concern and intrigue. My heart ached with the burden of deception, yet I knew I couldn't betray the trust placed upon me.

'So, I swallowed my truth, cloaking it in silence and vague reassurances. The work I did, the unseen battles fought, and the sacrifices made – these remained hidden in the shadowy recesses of my mind, locked away from her prying gaze. Despite her numerous attempts to peel back the layers of my secrets, I remained steadfast, a silent sentinel guarding the dark truths of our mission.'

'Okay, that's enough for now', Jim stated, his voice a mix of firmness and underlying tension, like the snap of a velvet-covered whip. He had tolerated the prying questions for a while, but there was a limit, a line that should not be crossed. With those words, it was as though he had dropped an iron curtain, creating an invisible but palpable barrier around himself.

Jim's eyes flickered with a hint of something indefinable – was it anger, hurt or merely a steely resolve? Whatever it was, it silenced the room. The air grew dense, charged with the weight of his unspoken, commanding nature. His private life was not merely personal; to him, it was a *sanctum sanctorum* – a sacred space that lay beyond the reach of casual curiosity and idle gossip. It was a place where the most intimate thoughts and experiences were kept, a fortress of solitude where only the most trusted could enter, if ever.

I felt the shift, an almost tangible pushback against my encroaching interest. My gaze dropped, the casual banter evaporating into awkward silence. It was clear that any further attempts to penetrate this boundary would be met not just with resistance but with a forceful rebuke – a reminder that some territories are meant to remain unexplored.

Jim's demeanour, usually open and affable, had transformed. There was a coldness now, a distant look in his eyes, as if he were peering into a place only he could see, a place where the noise of the world could not penetrate. His personal realm was a bastion of peace, where the chaos of outside judgments and expectations was kept at bay. It was where his true self lived, unfiltered and unobserved, and he guarded it with a vigilance that was as fierce as it was unyielding.

As the seconds ticked by, the weight of his words hung in the air, a lingering echo of his declaration. He didn't need to elaborate; the message was crystal clear. He was drawing a line, not just in conversation, but in the very fabric of our interaction. His private life was his own, and no amount of questioning or cajoling would ever breach those sacred walls.

The moment passed, but the impact of his statement lingered. The room, once vibrant with discussion, now felt like a hushed temple where an unspoken vow of silence had been imposed. I grappled with my thoughts, respecting the boundaries Jim had so resolutely set. We knew, from that point on, the sanctity of his private world was not to be trifled with. Jim had drawn his line in the sand, and it was clear – it would not be crossed.

'Have you been to see your parents recently?', I inquired, my voice tinged with curiosity and a hint of hesitation, unsure if the question would stir any deep emotions.

A serene smile spread across Jim's face, a glow of nostalgia lighting up his eyes. 'Oh yes', he replied, his voice carrying a wistful yet joyous tone. 'My mum and dad have created the most beautiful home in a hidden valley, nestled between rolling hills that are eternally green. It's a sanctuary where the air is always fresh, and the light dances through the leaves, creating patterns on the ground that look like something from a fairy tale.

'They're still together', Jim continued, a touch of reverence in his voice. 'After all these years, not once did they have to reincarnate. They're inseparable, like bread and butter, perfectly complementing each other in every way. My dad, with his gentle hands, has transformed their garden into a paradise. It's a riot of colours and scents, with flowers that seem to bloom endlessly and vines that climb and twine like they have a life of their own. He spends his days there, tending to each plant with the kind of love and care only he can give. And my mum', he added, his eyes softening with affection, 'she's found her haven here too. She still loves going to church, a little chapel that stands like a beacon of hope and peace in their valley. The bells toll softly, a call that echoes through the valley, gathering souls together. She has a wonderful social life here, surrounded by friends who share her warmth and kindness. They've created a community that feels like a family.'

He paused, as if savouring the memory, before continuing, 'It wasn't easy at first for them adjusting to this new plane of existence. The laws here are so different from what we were used to. But over time, they've found their rhythm. They've adapted and even thrived, making their life here just as beautiful as the one they left behind. It's like they were always meant to be here, in this tranquil, eternal place.' His words hung in the air, painting a picture so vivid and enchanting that I could almost see the valley and feel the gentle breeze on my skin.

'I must share with you a tale from beyond the veil of death, a narrative woven between my own passing and that of my parents. It revolves around Auntie Fay, a woman shrouded in mystery and eccentricity. Auntie Fay was an enigma, draped perpetually in a fur coat that exuded the pungent scent of mothballs. Her hat, oversized and a deep, earthy brown colour, sat atop her head like a crown of peculiar regality. She was the eldest of my mother's siblings, a sister who danced to a rhythm all her own – a rhythm that marked her as the odd one out in our family. A self-proclaimed spiritualist, Auntie Fay was deeply entrenched in the "otherworldly". She moved through life with an air of quiet conviction, claiming an unshakable connection with the ethereal realms. Her conversations were often punctuated with whispers of the afterlife, and she held an uncanny ability to commune with those who had crossed the threshold of mortality. To many, she was a figure of ridicule or skepticism, but to me, she was a beacon of intrigue and wonder.

'This story unfolds in the twilight zone between life and death, where Auntie Fay's presence became more than just an eccentric curiosity. It was there, in that shadowy borderland, that she reached out to me from beyond the grave. Her voice, clear and unwavering, carried the weight of secrets and the promise of revelations yet to come. In the lingering silence between breaths and heartbeats, Auntie Fay guided me through the mysteries of what lies beyond, offering glimpses into a world where the living and the dead coexist in a delicate balance.'

Jim laughed out aloud, and continued: 'Prepare yourself for a journey into the unknown, a venture into the mystical spaces where

Auntie Fay, with her peculiar attire and extraordinary gifts, navigated with the certainty of one who truly understood the unseen. This is not just a story of my Auntie Fay; it is a chronicle of the hidden connections between life, death and the uncanny pathways that lie in between.'

Jim paused, letting the weight of his words hang in the air before continuing. 'In the first book, I left out certain truths about myself and my family. There were secrets buried deep that were too painful and too profound to reveal. One such secret was the tale of Auntie Fay.

'My parents, staunch in their faith and unwavering in their devotion, were pillars of our local church community. They never missed a Sunday service and were often found baking cakes for the vicar, embodying the essence of dutiful parishioners. The thought of disturbing the dead or meddling with the supernatural was repugnant to them – completely at odds with their religious beliefs.

'When I passed over, their world was irrevocably shattered. The grief was a suffocating fog, and my death left a gaping void in their lives. Amidst their despair, Auntie Fay, with her mysterious ways and unconventional beliefs, emerged as an unexpected source of solace. She tried to share with her sister – my mum – her own spiritual convictions, but my mother's sorrow was a fortress, impenetrable to such notions.

'Yet Fay was relentless, her persistence a beacon of light in the darkness. Slowly, gently, she chipped away at my mother's resistance. She spoke of a place beyond the physical, a realm where the soul finds peace and where communication with the departed is possible. It was a concept my mother had always dismissed as sacrilege, but in the throes of her grief, desperation twisted the most steadfast of her convictions.

'It wasn't an overnight transformation. It was a gradual, almost imperceptible shift, but over time Fay's words began to resonate. The crushing weight of loss had made my mother seek comfort, wherever it might be found. Eventually, she found herself standing outside the doors of a Spiritualist church, her heart pounding with apprehension and hope. Inside, she encountered a world both strange and familiar, where the boundary between the living and the dead blurred, and where the promise of connecting with her lost son offered a glimmer of solace amidst the endless night of her grief.

'As Fay guided her sister into the bustling hall, they navigated through the sea of expectant faces, each person seemingly caught between hope and apprehension. The room buzzed with a mixture of quiet conversations and the rustling of programmes. Fay and her sister found two unoccupied seats near the back, slipping into them with an air of tentative comfort. Mum, fidgeting slightly, glanced around the unfamiliar surroundings, her eyes wide with curiosity and a hint of unease.

'The rostrum at the front of the hall was modestly elevated, spotlighting two figures. One was a composed, authoritative presence – the speaker for the evening. Next to him stood Mrs Jenkins, the medium. She was an older woman with an air of quiet confidence, her presence commanding without being overly imposing. The speaker introduced Mrs Jenkins as a clairvoyant, a vessel through which messages from the departed would flow. He spoke in measured tones, explaining that tonight the veil between the living and the dead would thin, and loved ones from beyond would reach out with words of comfort and guidance.

'As the introduction concluded, a hush fell over the hall. Anticipation hung thick in the air – the kind that made the room feel charged, almost electric. Fay noticed her sister clutching her handbag a little tighter, her knuckles white against the leather. It was clear that the notion of communicating with the afterlife was as alien as it was fascinating to her. The lights dimmed slightly, focusing all attention on the medium. Mrs Jenkins closed her eyes, taking a deep, deliberate breath, as if to gather strength from the ether. When she opened them again, her gaze seemed to pierce through the crowd, searching, seeking connections. For a moment, time seemed to stand still, and the only sound was the faint hum of the ceiling fans overhead. The audience collectively leaned forward, poised on the edge of their seats, waiting for the first message from beyond to break the silence.

'In the dimly lit room, Fay could feel the palpable mixture of hope, skepticism and longing emanating from the audience. She glanced at her sister, whose expression was now a blend of apprehension and guarded anticipation. The night promised to be a journey into the unknown – a dance between belief and doubt – as they waited for the veil to lift and the voices of the past to speak. The medium stepped forward, her gaze fixed on a young woman seated in the front row. Her voice, gentle yet laden with a profound intensity, cut through the hushed anticipation in the room. "My dear", she began, her eyes welling with a deep empathy, "I have made a connection with a soul very close to you."

'The young woman leaned in, her breath caught between hope and dread. "He's here with me now", the medium continued, her tone imbued with a reverence for the presence she was channelling. "He tells me his name is William, but you called him something special, didn't you? He remembers the nickname you gave him – Wannabe."

'At this revelation, the young woman's eyes widened, her hand flying to her mouth as tears began to flow freely. The room seemed to hold its breath, the weight of collective emotion pressing in. The medium's voice softened, becoming almost a whisper. "William wants you to know what happened", she said, her words hanging in the air like a delicate thread. "He tells me he went down on a hospital ship – a torpedo struck them."

'A gasp escaped from the young woman, her tears now a torrent as she trembled with the shock of finally knowing his fate. For so long, she had been left in a void of silence, his letters abruptly ceasing, leaving her in a state of anguished uncertainty. The medium took a deep breath, as if drawing strength from the spirit she was in contact with. "But my dear", she said, her voice trembling with the emotion of the moment, "William wants you to know he is at peace. He thanks you for all the love you gave him, for being his *beauty*."

'The young woman's sobs turned into a mixture of grief and relief, the poignant words filling the aching void in her heart. The room was enveloped in a profound silence; the only sound that could be heard was the quiet rustle of tissues and muffled weeping as others shared in her profound moment of closure and connection. The medium continued for the next hour giving very evidential messages to the public audience. "This will be my last message", she said, "before I finish."

'The room was dimly lit, shadows dancing along the walls from flickering lights. The anticipation was thick, an evident tension as the medium, a figure cloaked in an aura of mystique, surveyed the gathered audience. Her eyes, intense and piercing, scanned the crowd with an almost ethereal glow. Suddenly, she raised a hand, and her voice, hauntingly clear, broke through the silence, echoing to the far reaches of the hall.

'"You there, you with the brown hat on", she declared, her finger unwavering as it extended towards the back of the room. The audience collectively held their breath. My Auntie Fay, the woman in the brown hat, instinctively clutched her chest, feeling the weight of a hundred eyes. "Yes", she stammered, but the medium's gaze sharpened, slicing through Fay's hopeful reply. "No, not you", she corrected with a sombre inflection. "The woman next to you, who has just lost her son."

'The room seemed to freeze in time, a chill sweeping through mum, her face etched with the raw lines of grief. She whispered: "Yes, I've just lost my son." The medium closed her eyes briefly. I sensed her thoughts, asking me questions to prove who I am. She then opened her eyes, and her expression softened. "He wants you to know he never suffered much before passing over", she continued, her voice tender yet resonant, each word a lifeline to my grieving mother. "He's sorry for not listening to you, and he wants you to know that he loves you. He was with you when you went to church this morning and had tea with the vicar and friends. He's laughing now, saying he saw you spill your tea on the vicar's new rug."

'At those last words, the fragile dam holding back her sorrow burst. My mother's cries of anguish filled the hall, a heartbreaking symphony of loss and longing. "Jim, my darling son!", she wailed, her voice cracking with the unbearable weight of her grief. As the medium lowered her gaze, the room slowly began to stir from its spellbound state. The meeting came to a sombre close, the atmosphere heavy with emotion. Fay, eyes glistening with unshed tears, gently took her sister by the arm, guiding her through the throng of sympathetic murmurs.

'The tram ride home was a silent journey through a landscape of memories and heartache. Once inside the familiar walls of their home, Fay made tea, the act of boiling water and steeping leaves a small, comforting ritual amidst the chaos of sorrow. In the dimly lit kitchen, the atmosphere was heavy with unspoken emotions. The muted clink of porcelain cups against the wooden table and the steady, relentless ticking of the old wall clock were the only sounds punctuating the oppressive silence. Every tick seemed to amplify the quiet that enveloped them, a quiet that seemed to breathe with the weight of sorrow.

'Fay and mum sat side by side, the air thick with the grief that hung between them. The soft glow of the kitchen light cast long, overlapping shadows that danced lightly across their faces, tracing lines of worry and exhaustion. Fay's presence was more than mere companionship; it was a steadfast pillar of silent support. She remained close, her hand occasionally reaching out to gently touch her sister's, offering a wordless promise that she was not alone in this abyss of despair.

'The tea in their cups had long since cooled, but they continued to sip it slowly, finding a strange comfort in the familiar ritual. Each small sip was an act of shared endurance, a quiet rebellion against the encroaching darkness of their thoughts. The steam had dissipated, much like the day's warmth, leaving behind only the bitter strength of the brew – a fitting metaphor for the bitter strength they were both mustering.

'As they sat in the intimate cocoon of the kitchen, the world outside seemed distant and irrelevant. The night's chill began to creep into the room, but the warmth of their unspoken bond kept the cold at bay. They were each other's anchors, grounding one another in the tumultuous sea of their shared sorrow.

'Mum occasionally looked up, her eyes glistening with unshed tears, catching the sympathetic gaze of Fay. Each glance spoke volumes, conveying the depth of their grief and the solace they found in each other's presence. The silence between them was not empty but filled with the echoes of their shared history and the unbreakable ties of family love. In the corner of the kitchen, a small light flickered, casting a soft glow over a cosy armchair where Fay had settled in for the night. Her decision to stay over was a quiet, unassuming act of love and vigilance. She remained a silent sentinel, ready to step in if the gravity of the night's sorrow became too much to bear.

'As the minutes bled into hours, the kitchen became a haven of quiet resilience. The ticking clock, once a harsh reminder of passing time, now served as a comforting, rhythmic backdrop to their shared vigil. The weight of the day settled gently around them, not as a burden, but as a blanket of shared endurance. Together, they navigated the profound silence of the night, finding solace in each other's unwavering presence and the promise of facing the dawn together.

'Soon, both of them succumbed to the weariness that had been tugging at their eyelids. Mum slipped into her bed with the quiet caution of a burglar in the night, not daring to rustle the sheets or stir the air around Dad. She knew the weight of dawn's responsibilities and the world awaiting him at work come morning. But I stood vigil at Fay's bedside, my heart a heavy drumbeat echoing in the silent room. Shadows danced around us, weaving a tapestry of stillness and farewell. I watched her fragile form, so pale and serene, as if the very essence of her being was already on the precipice of departure.

'As the minutes ticked by, I held my breath, feeling the raw edge of the moment slicing through the night. My fingers brushed lightly against her hand, a touch so gentle it was almost imperceptible, a silent thank you for the unwavering strength she had shown Mum during those darkest hours. Then, with a whisper of a sigh, Fay's spirit began its journey beyond the veil, leaving behind only the faintest trace of her presence. I stood there, rooted to the spot, overwhelmed by the profundity of her silent support and the poignant beauty of her night-time release from her body – yet soon she would venture back to her body to start another day.

'I returned back to my world with a sense of both relief and trepidation, unsure of what awaited me. As I stepped into the familiar surroundings, there he was – Chan, standing amidst the shadows like a sentinel of my past. His voice cut through the silence like a blade, sharp and loaded with meaning. "Well", he remarked, his tone carrying a blend of curiosity and skepticism. "Are you happy now?"

'His words hung in the air, heavy with implications that reached far beyond the mere question. It wasn't just about my happiness – it was about the choices made, the paths taken, and the consequences faced. The tension between us crackled, echoing the unresolved complexities of our shared history. I met his gaze squarely, feeling the weight of every moment leading up to this encounter. The silence stretched, pregnant with unspoken truths and unfinished business. In that fleeting moment, the world seemed to hold its breath, as if waiting for my response to define the course of what lay ahead.

'After what felt like an eternity, I took a deep breath and gathered every ounce of courage that had eluded me for so long. The silence was suffocating, thick with unspoken tension. My heart pounded in my chest, a relentless drumbeat against the quiet. I could feel the weight of Chan bearing down on me, his expectations pressing like heavy stones on my shoulders. Summoning the strength I had long thought lost, I finally opened my mouth to speak. My voice trembled, the words almost sticking in my throat as I forced them out.

'"I'm sorry", I began, my voice barely above a whisper, yet it cut through the silence like a knife. "I shouldn't have visited my parents. I got caught up in all their dramas, and it was wrong of me." I paused, my eyes glistening with unshed tears as the memories of those tumultuous days flooded back. I continued, my voice gaining a bit of steadiness: "It ended up being good for my mum. Somehow, out of all that chaos, something positive came through for her."

'The room remained silent, the weight of my confession hanging in the air. My heart was still racing, but a sense of relief began to wash over me, knowing I had finally spoken the truth. Chan's tone was both compassionate and stern as he looked at me, his eyes reflecting a blend of wisdom and concern. "I do understand, Jim", he began, each word carefully measured. "Your curiosity and eagerness are commendable, and they show a spirit that is eager to learn and explore. However, my concern lies with your welfare. You are still very new to this realm, and the forces that permeate it are far more complex and unpredictable than you might realize."

'I shifted uneasily, feeling the weight of Chan's words. The *realm* Chan referred to was unlike anything I had ever experienced. It was a place where thoughts could shape reality, and unseen energies played out in a constant dance, affecting everything and everyone within it. I had recently found myself drawn into this world, a novice thrust into a field of infinite possibilities and equally infinite dangers.

'Chan continued, his voice steady and reassuring: "In this stage of your journey, you remain particularly vulnerable to the lower astrals. These are not physical entities but rather energies and influences that exist at a lower vibrational frequency. They are attracted to those who are new and inexperienced, seeking to feed off their uncertainty and fear. These astral entities can disrupt your progress, confuse your thoughts, and even pose a threat to your mental and spiritual well-being."

'My eyes widened as I took in Chan's words. I had heard whispers and read snippets about the lower astrals – forces that lurked at the periphery of human perception, waiting for an opportunity to exploit those who were unprepared. But hearing Chan speak about them with such seriousness made the threat seem far more real and immediate.

'"Your desire to explore the earth plane again is understandable", Chan acknowledged, his gaze softening as he saw the determination in my eyes. "But you must recognize that until you have developed sufficient mental strength and discipline, it is dangerous to venture there without protection. The earth plane, while familiar, is also fraught with its own set of challenges and energies that can be overwhelming if you're not prepared."

'I nodded slowly, digesting the gravity of Chan's advice. I remembered my last encounter on the earth plane – a vivid, almost surreal experience that had left me both exhilarated and deeply unsettled. The pull to return was strong, but so was the memory of the disorienting forces I had encountered. Chan's voice brought me back to the present. "It's crucial that you either have someone with you who can provide protection or wait until you have honed your mental defences sufficiently. Building this strength is not just about learning to shield yourself from external threats, but also about understanding and mastering your own internal landscape. Only then will you be able to navigate the complexities of both this realm and the earth plane with confidence and safety."

'I took a deep breath, feeling a mixture of frustration and gratitude. I appreciated Chan's concern and I knew that Chan's advice came from a place of deep understanding and care. Yet the yearning to explore and understand more of these realms burned within me. "I understand, Chan", I said finally, my voice tinged with resolve. "I'll take your advice to heart. I'll focus on building my strength and learning more about these forces. When I'm ready, I'll return to the earth plane. But for now, I'll proceed with caution and respect for the dangers you've described."

'Chan nodded approvingly, a small smile playing at the corners of his mouth. "Good. Remember, this journey is not a race. Each step you take, every bit of strength you gain, will prepare you for the vastness of what lies ahead. And know that you are not alone in this; I am here to guide and support you every step of the way." With those words, a sense of calm and clarity settled over me. I knew there was much to learn and many challenges to face, but with Chan's guidance and my own growing resilience, I felt ready to embrace the journey ahead.'

I now took the opportunity to intervene. 'Jim', I said, my voice laden with exhaustion, 'that's some story for the day, but I do need to rest now.'

Jim looked at me, a hint of concern in his eyes. 'I understand', he said gently, 'your body needs sustenance.' His voice seemed to echo through the quiet office, filled with unspoken sympathy. As he turned to leave, his words lingered in the air, a sombre reminder of my own frailty. I pushed myself up from my desk, the weight of fatigue pressing down on me. The chair creaked as I slid it back, its familiar sound a stark contrast to the silence that followed Jim's departure.

The office, usually a hive of activity, felt like a deserted cavern. Each step towards the door seemed to take an eternity, the distance stretching impossibly. I reached for the doorknob, my fingers brushing against the cold metal, and a shiver ran through me. The day's events had drained me, leaving me an empty shell. Once outside, the dim light of the hallway seemed almost blinding. I moved slowly, each step a struggle, feeling as if the world was spinning around me.

I managed to make my way to the bedroom, the bed beckoning like a siren call. As I lay down, the cool sheets embraced me, pulling me into their comforting depths. Sleep took me almost immediately – a heavy, dreamless slumber. Time lost all meaning; hours, minutes, seconds – they all blended into an unbroken void.

I was abruptly pulled from the abyss by the sound of the bedroom door creaking open. My eyes fluttered open to the dim light of the room, and I saw my partner standing there, her silhouette outlined by the fading twilight. 'Hi', she whispered, her voice a soft balm to my weary soul. 'Are you okay?'

I struggled to find my voice, managing only a weak grunt. 'Yes, sure', I mumbled, the words slurring together. Her presence was a comfort, a beacon of normalcy in my foggy consciousness. I drifted back into sleep, my partner's gentle presence fading into the darkness. The world outside ceased to exist, and I succumbed once more to the deep, unrelenting sleep that claimed me until the first light of dawn broke through the curtains, heralding a new day.

9

Ghostly Impressions

As I slowly emerged from the cocoon of my warm bed, the morning light spilled through the curtains, painting a hopeful glow across the room. I took a deep breath, savouring the crisp, invigorating air. I felt a surge of anticipation thrumming through my veins. Today wasn't just any ordinary day; it felt different, charged with a newfound energy. The air itself seemed to hum with possibilities.

As I stretched and rubbed the sleep from my eyes, a deep sense of contentment washed over me. I turned my head and my eyes fell on the familiar, cherished sight that made my heart swell with warmth – my partner. She was finally home, peacefully asleep beside me, after days of being away on her travels.

Her presence filled the room with a serene sense of completeness, a missing piece of my life's puzzle perfectly slotted back into place. I could see the gentle rise and fall of her chest, hear the soft whisper of her breath. It was as if her mere presence had banished the shadows that had lingered in the corners of my mind during her absence.

With a smile tugging at the corners of my lips, I gently slipped out of bed, careful not to wake her. The prospect of the day ahead felt bright and full of promise. Her return had rekindled a flame of optimism within me, and I was ready to embrace whatever the day had in store with open arms. This day, I felt, would be a tapestry woven with joy and the simple, profound happiness of having her back home.

I began the day with my customary morning ablutions, each step a ritualistic cleansing of the previous day's residue. The bathroom was filled with the fresh scent of minty toothpaste and the soothing warmth of a steaming shower. Revitalized, I made my way downstairs, the creak of each wooden step echoing in the quiet morning stillness. The kitchen welcomed me like an old friend, bathed in the soft, golden light of the early sun, streaming through the window.

I flicked on the kettle, its gentle hum a familiar background score to my waking thoughts. Today, however, I felt an unusual hunger gnawing at me, a reminder of last night's missed meal. Toast would not suffice. No, today I craved something more indulgent. I rolled up my sleeves and set to work, the kitchen slowly transforming into a haven of sizzling aromas and comforting warmth.

Before long, a full cooked breakfast was spread out before me: golden-brown sausages, crisp bacon, fluffy scrambled eggs, juicy grilled tomatoes, and hearty slices of toast slathered with butter. The *pièce de résistance*, a steaming cup of hot tea, sat beside the feast, its fragrant steam curling upwards in delicate tendrils. I savoured each bite, the flavours mingling together in a symphony of satisfaction.

Once my hunger was sated and the last crumb had been devoured, I took a moment to bask in the afterglow of my culinary creation. But the day was calling. I cleared away the remnants of my meal, each clink and clatter of dishes a prelude to the task ahead.

With the kitchen restored to its pristine state, I made my way to my sanctuary, my office. There, the blank pages awaited my pen's eager dance. Today, Jim and I would continue our journey, venturing deeper into the story that had captured my imagination. The familiar anticipation of writing buzzed within me as I settled into my chair, ready to craft the next chapter of our adventure.

A sudden shiver coursed through me, rippling down my spine like an electric current. The room, which had been warm just a moment ago, seemed to grow colder. I knew Jim was here. His presence enveloped me, tangible and comforting in the eerie stillness. 'Are you feeling better today?' His voice, deep and resonant, broke through the silence. It was a voice that could have belonged to a guardian angel or a spirit protector, but it was undeniably Jim – gentle and full of concern.

I turned to him, my eyes searching for his familiar face in the dim light. 'Yes, thank you', I managed to say, my voice trembling with the remnants of my earlier fright. 'I didn't realize how tired I was until my head hit the pillow.' As the words left my lips, I felt a wave of exhaustion wash over me once more, as if acknowledging my weariness gave it new power. I could still feel the faint, ghostly impression of the bed's embrace, the sensation of sinking into oblivion.

Jim's eyes softened, understanding and compassionate, as if he could see the shadows under my eyes, the burdens I carried. His presence was a balm to my frayed nerves. I felt a surge of gratitude and something deeper, something unspoken that lingered between us.

Outside, a heavy storm had erupted, the wind howled – a mournful symphony that matched the swirling emotions within me. I knew Jim's concern was genuine, his question more than just a polite inquiry. It was a lifeline, a thread connecting me to him in the vast, echoing expanse of my fatigue. For a moment, the world outside faded away. There was only Jim and the steady cadence of his breath, a rhythm that grounded me. I drew strength from his presence, feeling the cold ebb away, replaced by comforting warmth.

I met his gaze, letting the connection between us deepen. 'I'm glad you're here', I whispered, my voice barely audible over the storm that raged outside. And in that fleeting instant, I felt a sense of peace, as if the turbulence within and without had been stilled by the simple act of being together.

'Sit still', he commanded, his voice firm yet soothing, like a gentle thunderclap amidst the raging storm outside. The room dimmed, shadows stretching as the tempest's fury played against the walls. Jim's eyes, piercing and steady, locked onto mine, holding me captive. He raised his hands, hovering just inches above my head. An intense tension hung in the air, charged and electric. In that moment, the world outside seemed to sync with his intentions; the howling wind and crashing thunder mirrored the tumultuous energy gathering in his fingertips.

Suddenly, a torrent of warmth and light surged from his hands, an invisible cascade of raw power that hit me like a bolt of lightning. The force was overwhelming: an intoxicating wave that flooded through me, lighting up every nerve, igniting my very soul. It was as if the storm outside had entered my being, its energy coursing through my veins with a ferocity that I could barely comprehend. For a heartbeat, time stood still. The room pulsed with an otherworldly glow, and my senses exploded, overwhelmed by the sheer intensity of the experience. The tempest within me roared – an echo of the chaos outside – before it all abruptly ceased.

Jim lowered his hands, his gaze never wavering. The room fell silent, the storm's rage fading to a distant murmur. He leaned in closer, his voice a soft rumble, 'How do you feel now?' He stood there, his eyes twinkling with a mixture of mischief and modesty. The room was quiet – the kind of silence that follows a profound revelation. I took a deep breath, still processing the transformation I felt coursing through me.

'Well', I began, my voice trembling with gratitude and disbelief, 'what could I say except thank you?' The words barely escaped my lips before Jim's face lit up with a knowing smile.

'It's nothing', he shrugged nonchalantly, though his eyes betrayed a flicker of pride. 'Just a little trick I stumbled upon.'

I shook my head, overwhelmed by the sheer simplicity and power of his discovery. 'Trick or no trick, Jim', I insisted, my voice now steady and resolute, 'I feel amazing. It's like a fog has lifted, and for the first time I can see the path ahead clearly.' Jim's smile widened, but he remained silent, allowing me to soak in the moment. I could feel the inspiration bubbling up inside me, an unstoppable force ready to burst forth.

'I'm ready to write', I declared with newfound conviction. 'To pour out every thought, every idea, every word that has been trapped inside me. Thank you, Jim. Truly.' Jim nodded, his eyes softening as he watched me.

'Then go', he said quietly, almost reverently. 'Write. Let the world hear our voices.'

With those words, the room seemed to shimmer with possibility. I turned away, heart pounding with excitement and purpose, ready to unleash today's story upon the world.

'What better start than you explaining the mechanism of what you just did for me?', I said with a cheeky smile.

'It seems I've let myself in for this. I'll try to explain, what you call the mechanism', began Jim. 'So let's start with what most people on earth know of this subject: the concept of passing energy from one person to another is often discussed in various contexts; it's not new, Stephen. In cellular activity, every cell in our body generates electrical currents due to the movement of ions across cell membranes. This is fundamental to processes like muscle contractions and neural signalling. The heart's electromagnetic field generates the largest electromagnetic field in the body, much stronger than that of the brain. This field can be measured several feet away from the body using sensitive instruments. Our brain waves, with its electrical activity, produces different types of waves (alpha, beta, delta, etc.), detectable through electroencephalography (EEG), or by a psychic who can perceive radiations produced by the human body.

'In ancient Hindu and Buddhist traditions, chakras are centres of spiritual power in the human body, and are connected by channels of energy called *nadis*. Each chakra is associated with different aspects of physical and spiritual health, and their flows of energies. Meridians are pathways through which vital energy (Qi) flows. Acupuncture and acupressure are based on manipulating these energy flows to maintain health. Chan is a dab hand at this form of healing!

'Many spiritual traditions describe an aura, an energy field that surrounds the body. This field reflects the physical, emotional and spiritual state of a person. Our bodies generate energy through physical activities. Exercise, for instance, can enhance the flow of energy and create a sense of vitality. Then we come to concentration and mindfulness, these practices can influence the brain's electromagnetic activity, potentially affecting the body's overall energy field.

'This leads us on to emotional states. Emotions have a profound impact on our energy levels – "Energy in motion". Positive emotions like love and joy can enhance our energy fields, while negative emotions like anger and fear can disrupt them. Interconnectedness brings us to spiritual teachings which suggest that our energy fields connect us to the universe and to each other. This interconnectedness means that the energy we emit can affect not only ourselves but also those around us. Recognizing ourselves as powerhouses of energy can inspire a deeper understanding of our potential. Practices like meditation, yoga and Qigong are often aimed at harnessing and optimizing this inner energy.

'Our whole being is based on self-healing and growth: healing modalities such as Reiki, therapeutic touch and energy healing are based on the idea that manipulating the energy fields can promote physical, emotional and spiritual healing. Stephen, for over fifty years you have been practising healing – by now you should have worked out how it works?'

'I have a good idea', I replied, 'but let's carry on with your account.'

'Engaging in practices that align and enhance our energy fields can lead to greater health and well-being,' Jim continued. 'Meditation, for instance, is shown to alter brain-wave patterns and reduce stress. This is a fact – we are taught how to meditate properly here. Yoga and Tai chi are examples of physical practices that integrate movement with breath and focus, believed to balance and enhance the body's energy flow. Positive thinking and emotional resilience are not just beneficial for mental health but also for maintaining a strong, balanced energy field. Practices like 'gratitude journalling' or 'loving-kindness meditation' can enhance the heart's electromagnetic field, fostering a greater sense of connection and well-being.

'Many holistic health practices in your world today focus on the energy aspects of the body. Acupuncture, for example, aims to unblock energy pathways to restore balance and health. Integrating these practices with conventional medicine can provide a more comprehensive approach to health and wellness. Becoming aware of our own energy fields can lead to greater self-understanding and empathy. By tuning in to our own energy and the energy of others, we can cultivate deeper connections and more harmonious relationships. Practices like aura reading or 'energy scanning' can help individuals become more attuned to subtle energies.

'The idea that we are generators of immense energy aligns with many spiritual paths that emphasize personal growth and enlightenment. By cultivating our inner energy, we can pursue higher states of consciousness and spiritual fulfilment. Exploring this concept can lead to a deeper sense of purpose and a more profound connection with the universe.

'In summary, Stephen, viewing human beings as powerhouses generating immense electrical fields of energy offers a rich and multifaceted perspective on our existence. It bridges the gap between science and spirituality, encouraging a holistic view of health, consciousness and our place in the universe. This understanding invites us to explore and cultivate our inner energy, recognizing its potential to transform ourselves and our world. Now, this is the version you learned on the physical plane'. Jim's voice was low and resonant, echoing through the dimly lit room. He paused, the weight of his words hanging in the air. 'But it's a different story altogether when you cross over to my side of life.'

Jim's eyes, normally vibrant and expressive, took on a distant, glazed look as he spoke, as if he were glimpsing into a realm beyond our reality, where ordinary logic didn't apply. The temperature in the room seemed to drop, sending a chill through me, and I found myself holding my breath, caught in a grip of uneasy anticipation. 'You see', he continued, his voice now barely above a whisper, 'on this side, we grasp only fragments, like echoes of a melody. But over there, on the other side, where I dwell now, everything shifts. The rules, the very fabric of existence, are not just bent; they are shattered and rebuilt in ways you can't even begin to fathom.'

The desk light cast eerie shadows on the walls, dancing to the cadence of his words. A heavy silence fell, as if the world itself had stopped to listen – to understand the depths of what Jim was revealing. There was a sense of something unseen, something vast and incomprehensible lurking just beyond the veil of reality.

Jim's gaze seemed to pierce through me, his eyes filled with a mixture of sorrow and profound understanding. 'When you come to my side of life, you don't just learn the truth – you become it. And the version of the story you thought you knew – it unravels, revealing the tapestry of a universe far more intricate and mysterious than you could ever imagine.' He stopped speaking, but his presence lingered, a ghostly reminder of the thin line between the world of the living and the realm beyond. The room remained silent. I was grappling with the weight of his revelation, wondering about the unseen worlds that lay just out of reach, and the profound mysteries that awaited me there.

'Try to understand, Stephen' – Jim's voice was heavy with a mixture of earnestness and an eerie calm, as though he were revealing a forbidden secret. 'When you die, your physical body, the one you've known all your life, is left behind on Earth. It is destined to return to the elements, dissolving back into the soil, the water and the air from which it originated. It's not just a body that you shed; it's an entire world of sensations, of weight, of boundaries and limitations. You cease to exist in the material form you've always understood.

'In death, your journey is far from over. You move into a new realm, one where the constraints of the physical world no longer bind you. Here, your being is transformed, reconstructed from astral elements – subtle, elusive and profoundly different from the coarse matter that once defined you. This astral body is not tangible in the way your earthly form is. It is composed of energies that are both intricate and ethereal, connecting you more deeply to the cosmos' fundamental forces.

'Imagine it like a butterfly emerging from a chrysalis, but infinitely more profound. Your physical body was merely a vessel, a temporary shell, and upon death you leave this shell behind. The new form you take on is like a delicate yet powerful spirit, crafted from the very essence of the universe's most mystical and intangible energies. The energy that sustains this new form is vastly different from the physical nourishment your old body required. It is drawn from the astral plane, where the rules of our earthly existence no longer apply. This energy is akin to a fine, shimmering light that feeds and nurtures your new essence. It is a force of pure, unbounded vitality, resonating with the frequencies of the cosmos itself. In this state, you are no longer constrained by the physical limitations that once held you. You become a part of something greater, connected to the infinite web of existence. The transformation is both exhilarating and daunting, as you let go of the familiar and embrace the boundless, navigating a realm where time and space as we know them cease to exist.

'So, when you die, Stephen, it's not an end, but a profound shift into a higher state of being. You shed the tangible, the finite, and step into a dimension of pure energy and endless possibility. It's a journey into the unknown, where you are reborn as a creature of the astral, sustained by the very forces that move the stars and shape the universe.

'In the universe I inhabit, thought reigns supreme. It is the cornerstone, the essence that differentiates your world from mine. While your world is bound by tangible laws, rigid structures and immutable realities, my world is an ethereal expanse where the boundaries of the mind dissolve, giving way to an endless sea of possibilities shaped by the currents of my thoughts. There, the power of thought is the ultimate sovereign. It transcends the physical constraints of your existence and wields the authority to craft and mould reality itself. With a mere whisper of intent, the abstract becomes tangible, the imagined becomes real. This is not a place where dreams are distant hopes; here, they are the very fabric of existence, interwoven with the threads of consciousness.

'In my world, the mental landscape is a living, breathing entity, ever-evolving with each fleeting idea and profound contemplation. The skies are painted with the hues of my desires, the ground firmed by the solidity of my beliefs. Mountains rise and fall with the ebb and flow of my will, oceans churn with the depths of my passion, and entire realms blossom from the seeds of a single thought.

'Your reality is a canvas restricted by the physical, governed by the laws of matter and time. But in my domain, thought is not just the artist's brush; it is the palette, the canvas and the muse. It is a realm where the act of thinking is an act of creation, where every mental whisper can summon worlds into existence or dissolve them into oblivion. This mental dominion is a place of profound freedom and terrifying responsibility. Here, the consciousness is unbound, capable of infinite creation and boundless exploration. Yet with such power comes the weight of its wielding. Every thought must be nurtured with care, for in this realm the merest flicker of the mind can ignite fires of creation or storms of destruction.

'In your world, thought is often an internal process, unseen and unheard. But in mine, it is the heartbeat of reality, the very force that shapes and drives existence. It is the divine spark, the god-like force that distinguishes my world from yours – a realm where the mind does not merely interpret reality but commands it into being. Thus, the power of thought is the divine factor that separates your reality from my own. It is the foundation upon which my world stands – a mental empire where imagination knows no bounds, and every thought is a decree that shapes the very essence of existence. Therefore, I possess the extraordinary ability to instantly attune myself to the precise frequency required to amplify not only my own electrical field but also that of others. This unique skill is a vital part of our training, an essential technique we rescuers are meticulously taught before we descend into the perilous lower realms. Our mission?

To engage in fierce combat with the sinister entities of the lower astrals. It's not just a lesson; it's a transformative rite of passage that prepares us to harness the raw, potent energy needed to confront and vanquish the dark forces that lurk in those treacherous depths.

'This attunement is our lifeline, our shield and our weapon in the relentless battle against the encroaching shadows. Imagine plunging into a world where darkness reigns – a place where the air thrums with malevolent intent. The lower realms are not for the faint of heart; they are a labyrinth of despair, filled with the tortured wails of lost souls and the relentless, insidious whispers of the astral beings who thrive on fear and chaos. In these forsaken places, the ability to adjust our frequencies becomes crucial. It allows us to forge an invisible yet unbreakable connection with the life force that courses through every living being. This connection grants us the power to stabilize, heal and protect those who are vulnerable to the astrals' corrupting influence. It's akin to tuning a delicate instrument, where even the slightest miscalibration can lead to disaster.

'The training is rigorous, demanding unwavering focus and mental fortitude. We spend countless hours in meditation, learning to sense and manipulate the subtle energies that permeate our universe. We practise under extreme conditions, simulating the oppressive darkness and the overwhelming presence of the lower realms until our responses become instinctual. Only then are we deemed ready to face the real threat.

'The battles we fight are not always visible to the naked eye, but they are no less real. When we confront an astral being, it is a clash of wills and energies, a struggle that transcends the physical realm. The frequency attunement enables us to repel their attacks, dismantle their ethereal forms, and ultimately, to restore balance to the realm. Each successful mission reinforces the importance of our training and the power of our abilities. The attunement becomes second nature, a part of who we are as rescuers. It is our legacy, passed down through generations – a testament to our enduring commitment to protect and heal. We are the guardians of the light, standing resolute against the encroaching darkness, ever ready to descend into the depths to safeguard the sanctity of the realms.

'Therefore, Stephen, the act of channelling my energy to you is not only a simple task for me, but it also brings profound benefits to you. The transfer of this life force flows effortlessly through me, like a river descending from the highest peaks, powerful and unstoppable. As it reaches you, it invigorates your very soul, infusing you with a vitality and strength that transcends mere physical rejuvenation. This exchange is a gift, a blessing that will ignite your spirit and illuminate the path ahead of you, allowing you to achieve greatness beyond your wildest dreams.'

We both laughed out loud, the kind of laughter that starts deep in your belly and rolls out uncontrollably, echoing off the walls. Tears pricked the corners of my eyes, and my sides ached with the sheer force of it. Jim had that effect on people; his wit was sharp as a tack, and he always knew just the right thing to say to crack me up.

'Okay, okay', I managed to gasp between bouts of laughter, holding up a hand in mock surrender. 'But seriously, I need a toilet break. All this laughing has made it impossible to ignore the urgent call of nature!' I doubled over, clutching my stomach, feeling an unexpected but unmistakable pressure building up. It was like the laughter had shaken loose something inside me, and now there was no stopping it. I dashed towards the restroom, leaving Jim still chuckling behind me.

As the afternoon light began to fade, casting long shadows across my study, I seized the moment to escape the mounting tension. I took the opportunity to make myself a steaming cup of aromatic tea, the comforting scent wafting through the room like a gentle embrace. Alongside the tea, I carefully selected a few delicate biscuits, their crisp edges promising a satisfying crunch. I did not offer any of this to Jim. How could I? You understand the reason, don't you? Jim, who stood across from me in the dim light, was beyond the reach of such earthly pleasures. His spectral presence, though barely visible, carried an undeniable weight that chilled the air between us.

With my modest feast in hand, I returned to my desk. The warm glow of the lamp pooled over my computer. Settling back into my chair, I took a sip of the hot tea, letting its warmth seep into me. Then, with a measured tone, I broke the silence. 'Jim', I asked, my voice soft yet steady, 'do you miss food and drink?' The question hung in the air, pregnant with the unspoken understanding that his response would pull us both deeper into the realm of the unknown, where the living and the departed momentarily converge. Jim's gaze, a mixture of nostalgia and melancholy, met mine. He seemed to ponder the question, as if searching for the right words to describe an existence that defied the earthly senses. After a moment, he began to speak, his voice carrying the weight of memories and experiences long past.

'It's not quite like that', Jim said slowly, choosing his words with care. 'The sensation of hunger, the taste of a favourite meal, the pleasure of a cold drink on a hot day – those are things tied to the physical body. And my body, as you know, is no longer my home.' He paused, his eyes drifting as if he were seeing a world beyond our own. 'But I do remember', he continued, a faint smile touching his lips. 'I remember the joy of a family dinner, the comfort of Mum's homemade soup when I was sick, the simple pleasure of sharing a drink with friends. Those memories are vivid, almost as if they were imprinted on my soul.'

I leaned in, intrigued by his perspective. 'So you don't experience hunger or thirst anymore?'

Jim shook his head. 'No, not in the way the living do. But there is a kind of longing, I suppose. Not for the physical act of eating or drinking, but for the connections those acts represent – the togetherness, the sense of belonging. That's what I missed. The rituals, the moments that made me feel alive.'

His words hung in the air, resonating with a truth that transcended our different planes of existence. I took another sip of my tea, feeling the weight of his revelation. 'It sounds like those moments were really important to you.'

'They were', Jim agreed. 'They still are, in a way. Even though I can't partake in them anymore, the memories sustain me. They remind me of who I was, and in some ways, who I still am. It's a different kind of nourishment – one that feeds the soul rather than the body.' As he spoke, I felt a sense of peace settle over the room. Jim's presence, though no longer physical, was undeniably real. His memories, his emotions, his essence – they all lingered, weaving a tapestry of a life that had once been and still, in some ethereal form, continued to be.

'Thank you for sharing that with me, Jim', I said softly. 'It means a lot to hear your side of the story.'

He nodded, his smile growing warmer. 'Thank you for listening. It's nice to be remembered and to know that my story isn't over, even if it's taken a different turn.' With that, the room fell silent once more, but the silence was now filled with a deeper understanding, a connection that bridged the gap between our worlds. I took another sip of my tea, savouring the warmth, and felt a profound sense of gratitude for the moment we had just shared.

'What happens to those who struggle to adapt to the conditions of the astral plane they now find themselves in?'

Jim began to explain: 'Those who find themselves unable to adjust to the conditions of the astral plane may experience a range of disconcerting and often unsettling consequences. The astral plane, with its ever-shifting landscapes and ethereal forms, demands a certain degree of adaptability and understanding that not all souls possess upon arrival. As the newly transitioned soul steps into the astral plane, they are met with an overwhelming array of vivid colours, swirling energies and the lingering echo of countless thoughts. The very fabric of this realm is in constant flux, responding to the subtle currents of emotion and intention. For those unprepared, this can be a harrowing experience.

'Some souls, disoriented and bewildered, find themselves lost in a maze of their own creation. Their fears and anxieties manifest as tangible obstacles – dark, twisting corridors filled with shadows that whisper their deepest insecurities. These souls may wander aimlessly, trapped in a cycle of their own making, unable to see beyond the phantoms of their mind. Others might experience a profound sense of isolation. The astral plane, though teeming with life and energy, can feel desolate to those who cannot perceive its nuances. They might feel adrift in a vast, empty expanse, where the silence is deafening and the absence of familiar anchors is stark. This isolation can lead to a deep, existential loneliness, as they struggle to connect with the beings and energies around them. In more extreme cases, some souls might be drawn to dark and chaotic regions of the astral plane, areas where negative energies and malevolent entities reside. These souls, unable to shield themselves or navigate away, can become entangled in tumultuous storms of psychic energy. Here, they may face relentless torment as they are buffeted by waves of despair and fear, their own unresolved traumas and regrets magnified and reflected back at them in an endless, nightmarish loop.

'There are also those who resist the nature of the astral plane, clinging stubbornly to their earthly perceptions and beliefs. This resistance creates a dissonance, a rift between their soul and the flow of the astral energies. They may experience intense confusion, as the reality they try to impose does not align with the fluidity of the astral realm. This can result in a painful fragmentation of their identity, as their rigid constructs are continuously shattered by the realm's inherent dynamism.

'However, all is not lost for these struggling souls. Guides and benevolent entities, attuned to the sufferings of the newly arrived, often extend their aid. These guiding spirits may appear as familiar faces, comforting presences, or radiant beings of light, offering gentle guidance and support. Through patient assistance, they help these souls gradually acclimatize, teaching them to release their fears, open their perceptions and embrace the boundless possibilities of the astral plane. In time, even the most disoriented souls can learn to navigate this new existence, finding their place within the intricate tapestry of the astral realm. Their journey, though fraught with challenges, becomes a path of profound transformation and self-discovery, as they come to understand the true nature of their consciousness and the limitless potential that lies within.

'What happens, Stephen, is quite dramatic and often unexpected. If the lower astral entities succeed in persuading the newly deceased to follow them – under the guise of showing them the ropes in this new and bewildering plane – the situation can become startling and even perilous. These entities, often mischievous and sometimes malevolent, take these souls to places that closely resemble the pleasures and distractions of the physical world they have just left behind. They lead them to places brimming with earthly temptations – pubs, restaurants and lively, joyous spots that mirror the indulgences they once knew and loved.

'Imagine, if you will, a soul newly freed from the constraints of its physical body, still carrying the memories and habits of its earthly life. This soul is bewildered, disoriented and desperately seeking familiarity in the strange new landscape of the astral plane. It is at this vulnerable moment that the lower astral entities strike. They approach the bewildered soul with false friendliness, offering guidance and companionship in an unfamiliar realm. They are cunning and persuasive, painting a picture of comfort and enjoyment that is hard to resist.

'The lower astral plane is a realm of illusion and deceit, a shadowy reflection of the material world. These entities take the souls to places designed to evoke memories and desires from their earthly existence. Pubs and restaurants appear almost identical to those they frequented in life, filled with the same sounds, smells, and even tastes. These places are traps, carefully crafted to anchor the souls to the lower astral plane by rekindling their earthly attachments. The appeal of these familiar pleasures can be overpowering. Imagine a soul that, in life, found solace in the camaraderie of a pub, the taste of a favourite meal, or the joy of a festive gathering. In the lower astral plane, these same pleasures are tantalizingly within reach, but they are mere shadows of the real thing. The soul, in its confusion, may fail to realize that these are illusions, meant to keep it bound to a lower vibrational state. The entities use these illusions to ensnare the souls, trapping them in a cycle of longing and attachment to the physical world they have just left behind.

'This entrapment can have severe consequences for the soul's journey. Instead of progressing to higher planes of existence, where true spiritual growth and enlightenment can occur, the soul becomes stuck in a limbo of sorts. It is caught in a web of desires and illusions, unable to move forward or fully let go of its earthly life. The lower astral entities, feeding off the energy of these imprisoned souls, grow stronger, perpetuating a cycle of entrapment and exploitation.

'However, not all is lost for them. There are forces of light and higher beings who work tirelessly to rescue and guide these lost souls towards the path of ascension. These benevolent entities strive to break the chains of illusion and desire, helping the souls to see through the deceit of the lower astral plane. They offer healing, comfort and true guidance, leading the souls away from the false pleasures and towards the light of higher realms. The key for these souls is to recognize the illusions for what they are, and to seek the higher truths that lie beyond. It is a journey of awakening and realization, of letting go of the attachments that bind them to the lower planes. With the help of higher beings and a renewed focus on spiritual growth, they can break free from the cycle of illusion and continue their journey towards enlightenment. In the end, what happens to those who cannot adjust to the conditions of the astral plane is a matter of choice and awareness. The temptations of the lower astral entities are strong, but the light of truth and higher consciousness is stronger. It is a battle between illusion and reality, between lower desires and higher aspirations. And it is a battle that, with the right guidance and inner strength, can be won.'

'Jim', I began – my voice tinged with curiosity and a hint of scepticism – 'you said there's no eating or drinking as we know it in that realm. So, when newcomers find themselves face-to-face with lower astral beings, how do they handle the need for sustenance?'

Jim leaned back thoughtfully before responding. 'It's fascinating, really. In the astral plane, beings don't have physical bodies like yours, so the concept of consuming food or drink in the traditional sense doesn't apply. Instead, interactions often involve exchanging energies, emotions, or even ideas. Lower astral beings, in particular, may still possess residual memories or habits from their time in physical form, leading them to simulate eating or drinking during encounters with newcomers. This can be confusing for those transitioning from the physical realm.'

Jim continued, his voice taking on a reflective tone. 'For new arrivals, the experience can vary widely depending on their awareness and state of consciousness. Some may perceive sensations akin to eating or drinking, driven by their expectations or beliefs. Others might not feel the need at all, finding sustenance through different forms of energetic exchange or simply adapting to the astral environment's unique dynamics.'

I nodded, absorbing the explanation. 'So, it's more about energy and perception than actual physical consumption?'

'Exactly', Jim affirmed, his demeanour earnest. 'Understanding the astral realm requires openness to new experiences and a willingness to redefine our understanding of existence beyond the physical body. It's a realm where consciousness plays a central role in shaping reality, including how beings interact and perceive each other.'

As Jim delved deeper into the topic, I found myself intrigued by the notion of a reality so fundamentally different yet intricately connected to our own. The concept of astral existence, with its blend of mystique and profound insight, sparked a newfound curiosity that lingered long after our conversation ended. But for now, Jim had some more to relay on the subject.

'In the shadowed depths of earthly pubs, where the air hangs heavy with the scent of stale ale and the murmur of drunken conversations fills the room, a clandestine drama unfolds. Here, amidst the dim glow of flickering lights dwell the crafty lower astrals. They prowl silently among the patrons, their ethereal forms cloaked in darkness as they survey the room with keen, otherworldly eyes. These lower astrals, beings of a realm unseen by mortal eyes, are drawn to the intoxicating aura of those who indulge heavily in drink. With a calculated gaze, they assess the vibrant energy fields, seeking out individuals whose frequencies resonate with their own insidious desires. In an impulsive decision fuelled by their primal instincts, they may choose to infiltrate and occupy the aura of a vulnerable human. Yet in the chaotic realm of the lower astrals, coveting a single host often sparks discord. More than one entity may crave dominion over the same soul, igniting a fierce struggle amidst the unseen shadows. A tumultuous battle ensues, a clash of wills and energies, echoing silently alongside the boisterous revelry of the pub.

'Amidst the haze of alcohol and the growing disarray within the astral plane, the strongest among the lower astrals prevails, seizing control over the human vessel. As the unsuspecting mortal succumbs further to intoxication, their energies shift and fluctuate, creating ripples that resonate through the interconnected web of astral realms. It is then that the lower astrals, now merged with their chosen host, begin to experience an unexpected transformation. The intoxicating effects of alcohol, coursing through the human's veins, manifest as vibrational changes in their ethereal forms. Sensations previously unknown to these astral beings now ripple through their essence, mirroring the inebriation of their earthly counterpart. Yet unbeknownst to these lower astrals, lurking in the shadows beyond their realm, exist beings more grotesque and malevolent. These entities feed voraciously upon the negative energies exuded by the lower astrals, siphoning off the discord and turmoil spawned by their clandestine battles. Thus, in the depths of the earthly pubs, where the boundaries between worlds blur beneath the veil of intoxication, a clandestine ballet unfolds: mortals unaware, lower astrals engaged in silent warfare, and darker entities lurking in anticipation – all intertwined in a dance of unseen forces, playing out amidst the flickering lights and the chorus of drunken revelry.

'Now I think, Stephen, you truly deserve a rest. Let's call it a day for now, and I shall see you bright and early in your morning', Jim declared with genuine concern in his voice.

Jim departed, leaving me to contemplate his words. As I prepared for my evening meal, thoughts of the lower astrals and their relationship with alcohol lingered uneasily in my mind. The comforting routine of pouring myself a glass of deep red wine was momentarily interrupted by Jim's cautionary tale. Perhaps, I thought to myself, it would be wise to reconsider that second glass of wine tonight.

My partner outdid herself with a magnificent lasagna that filled the house with an irresistible aroma. The layers of perfectly cooked pasta, rich meat sauce and creamy cheese melded together in a symphony of flavours that left me no choice but to indulge in a second helping. Every bite was a testament to her culinary skill, and I savoured each one with delight. To accompany this culinary masterpiece, I poured myself a single, well-deserved glass of exquisite red wine. Its robust flavour complemented the lasagna perfectly, enhancing the dining experience to a level of pure bliss.

After this delightful feast, we retreated to the cosy sanctuary of the lounge. The soft cushions of the sofa embraced us as we settled in to watch a movie. We opted for something light-hearted and comforting, steering clear of anything too scary. It was the perfect end to a perfect evening – a time of simple joy and contentment shared together.

10

Dreams

I was eager to start writing, despite the restless and turbulent night I had endured. My sleep had been plagued by unruly dreams that twisted and turned, leaving me exhausted and unsettled. These vivid nightmares seemed to be a direct result of yesterday's unnerving conversation with Jim about the lower astral beings.

As I sat at my desk, the memory of our dialogue haunted me. Jim's descriptions of these ethereal entities, their shadowy forms and malevolent intentions, had burrowed deep into my subconscious. The way he spoke, with a mixture of fear and fascination, painted a chilling picture that refused to leave my mind. Every time I closed my eyes, I was thrust back into a realm where these beings lurked in the corners of my dreams, their presence a constant, unsettling force. I could feel their eyes on me, sense their whispered threats. It was as if they were reaching out from the astral plane, trying to pull me into their dark world.

Despite this, my urge to write was unstoppable. There was a story within me, desperate to escape, and I couldn't let the fear of these otherworldly encounters hold me back. The keys of my computer clacked with a fierce determination, each stroke a defiant stand against the lingering dread. I resolved to channel the unsettling energy from my dreams into my writing, transforming my fear into creativity. The lingering terror from my nocturnal visions infused my words with an intensity I hadn't experienced before. I would not be defeated by these spectral entities; instead, I would harness the power of my imagination to conquer them.

With every sentence, I distanced myself from the grip of the lower astral beings, turning my fear into fuel for my craft. The act of writing became a cathartic release, a way to exorcise the demons that had haunted my sleep. In the end, my unruly dreams and the dark dialogue with Jim became the catalyst for my most compelling work yet.

A coarse, jarring 'Good morning' from Jim shattered my concentration, wrenching me back from the world of my writing. He loomed behind me, his brow furrowed with curiosity. 'What are you writing about?', he inquired, his tone laced with genuine interest.

I hesitated, the memories of the previous night still raw. 'Oh, I had a bad night', I began, my voice trembling. 'It was full of nightmares and stuff. That's all. I'm okay now, thank you.' I forced a smile, hoping to convey a sense of normalcy, though inside I felt anything but that.

'Well, shall we start?', Jim asked.

'Sure', I replied. 'Where do you want to go today?'

'Let's begin with what's been troubling you', Jim suggested. 'Let's talk about your dreams and nightmares.'

And so Jim began his dialogue: 'Dreams and nightmares have long fascinated humanity, serving as windows into our subconscious minds. They are intricate narratives woven by our brains, often blurring the line between reality and imagination. Dreams can be whimsical, bizarre or even prophetic, while nightmares plunge us into a world of fear and anxiety. Understanding these phenomena requires delving into the nature of sleep, the stages of dreaming, and the psychological and physiological factors that influence them.

'Dreams occur primarily during the Rapid Eye Movement (REM) stage of sleep, a phase characterized by heightened brain activity, similar to wakefulness. During REM sleep, the brain processes emotions, consolidates memories and engages in problem-solving. This stage typically recurs several times throughout the night, with each cycle lasting longer than the previous one, allowing for multiple dream experiences. Your dreams, Stephen, are a fascinating blend of reality and fantasy, often reflecting our waking life. They can incorporate elements from our daily experiences, emotions and even unresolved issues. Freud famously theorized that dreams are manifestations of our deepest desires and anxieties, often symbolized through various dream elements. Although modern psychology has moved beyond Freud's strict interpretations, it acknowledges that dreams can provide valuable insights into our subconscious minds.

'Nightmares are a darker counterpart to dreams, characterized by vivid, distressing imagery that can provoke strong emotional responses, such as fear, anxiety or sadness. They often occur during REM sleep and can jolt a person awake, leading to difficulty falling back asleep. Nightmares are common across all ages but are particularly prevalent in children. The causes of nightmares are multifaceted, ranging from psychological factors such as stress, anxiety, and trauma to physiological conditions like sleep disorders or medication side effects. Traumatic experiences, in particular, can lead to recurrent nightmares, a condition known as post-traumatic stress disorder (PTSD). Nightmares in PTSD are often direct replays of the traumatic event, underscoring the close link between our experiences and the content of our dreams.

'Dreams and nightmares provide a unique glimpse into our subconscious minds. They can act as a coping mechanism, allowing us to process emotions and experiences in a safe, symbolic manner. For instance, a person dealing with grief might dream of a lost loved one, providing a sense of closure or comfort. Similarly, nightmares can bring unresolved fears to the forefront, prompting us to address issues we might be avoiding in our waking life. From a neuroscientific perspective, dreams are a byproduct of the brain's efforts to make sense of neural activity during sleep. The brain's limbic system, which is involved in emotional processing, is particularly active during REM sleep, explaining why dreams often carry strong emotional content. The prefrontal cortex, responsible for logical reasoning and self-control, is less active, allowing for the bizarre and illogical nature of dreams.

'Throughout history, dreams have been regarded with a mixture of awe and curiosity. Ancient civilisations often saw dreams as messages from the gods or as omens. The Egyptians believed that dreams could predict the future, while the Greeks and Romans thought they were a way to communicate with the divine. Indigenous cultures around the world also hold rich traditions surrounding dreams, often using them as tools for guidance and healing.

'In modern times, dreams continue to captivate our imagination. The field of dream analysis, while not an exact science, has provided valuable tools for understanding the human psyche. Carl Jung, a contemporary of Freud, introduced the concept of archetypes and the collective unconscious, suggesting that certain symbols and themes recur across different cultures and individuals, pointing to a shared human experience. For those plagued by frequent nightmares, various coping strategies can be employed. Maintaining a regular sleep schedule, creating a relaxing bedtime routine and addressing sources of stress can help reduce the frequency of nightmares. Cognitive-behavioural therapy (CBT) and techniques like imagery rehearsal therapy (IRT) have proven effective in treating chronic nightmares, especially those stemming from PTSD.

'Dreams and nightmares are more than just fleeting experiences during sleep; they are profound reflections of our inner worlds. They offer a canvas where our deepest fears, desires and emotions play out, often providing valuable insights into our subconscious. Whether they leave us enchanted or terrified, dreams and nightmares remain a fundamental aspect of the human experience, continuing to intrigue scientists, psychologists and dreamers alike.'

'Jim, where on earth did you learn all this?'

'Stephen', Jim began, his voice taking on a mystical tone, 'I never learned all this in the conventional sense. Remember, I explained to you some time ago about one's ability to tap into an ancient library using the power of one's thoughts. Well, Chan taught me how to achieve this. The library in question is called the Akasha Library, a vast and timeless repository of knowledge and wisdom. All I do is connect with it, and I can access the information stored there. So, what I share with you isn't learned in the traditional way; it's read directly from the Akasha Library. That's all.'

'Can you show me how to do that?', I enquired rather hastily, my voice trembling with an eagerness I could barely contain.

Jim suddenly burst into laughter, a sound that echoed through the quiet room, its unexpected volume startling me. 'No, I'm sorry', he said, his tone shifting to one of solemnity as he continued. 'I can't. It takes an immense development of one's soul to achieve such a feat. The Akasha Library is not for the faint of heart; it opens its doors only to those who have refined themselves on both a mental and spiritual level. It is a sacred repository of knowledge, safeguarded by mechanisms beyond our comprehension.'

He paused, his eyes distant, as if recalling ancient memories. 'There have been a few extraordinary individuals – Tesla, Einstein and a handful of others – who possessed the unique ability to bypass these cosmic safeguards. These men were not just brilliant minds; they were beings of profound spiritual insight. To reach the Akasha Library is to transcend the ordinary and enter a realm where the ultimate prize of enlightenment awaits. It is not a path easily trodden.'

My downturned lips spoke volumes of my disappointment.

'Why are you looking so glum? The wonderful gifts of the spirit that God has bestowed upon you, Stephen, are marvels in themselves!', Jim exclaimed, his voice swelling with an almost reverent fervour. 'Think of the countless souls who have been touched by your healing hands over the past fifty years. Hundreds of thousands of people, each one leaving your clinic with a renewed sense of hope and a spirit rejuvenated by your touch.' He gestured around the room, his eyes wide with awe. 'Look at these walls! They are adorned with the extraordinary photographs capturing the divine light that manifests here, a testament to the miracles that happen within these very confines. The beautiful pink light that emanates from you during your healings, a phenomenon that defies explanation – these are not mere coincidences, Stephen. They are signs, powerful reminders of the spiritual force that flows through you.'

Jim stepped closer, his voice softening but losing none of its intensity. 'These gifts, these miracles, are not just for you – they are for the world. You are a conduit for the divine, a beacon of light in a dark world. Every smile, every tear of joy, every whispered "thank you" from those you have healed, are testaments to the incredible power within you. Embrace it, Stephen. The world needs your light now more than ever.'

'Well, when you put it that way, of course, I'm profoundly grateful. Just a few weeks ago, I had an incredibly enriching experience that reinforced my beliefs. I raised the kundalini energy twice in succession, which had never happened before. Not one after the other! As you know, Jim, my philosophy revolves around simplicity and authenticity. People often ask me which form of yoga is best to practise, and I always draw upon the wisdom of the ancient Indian masters. These sages spoke of our current era as the Kali Yuga, a dark age where human consciousness hit rock bottom. But, fortunately, we are now emerging from this nadir and entering a period of spiritual ascent.

'When I'm asked about the best yoga practice', I continued, 'I share the timeless guidance these masters offered ten thousand years ago. They emphasized the transformative power of Bhakti Yoga, which is essentially about falling deeply, madly in love with God. This practice transcends physical postures and rigid disciplines; it's about cultivating a heartfelt devotion and a profound, personal connection with the divine. It's about surrender, love and seeing the divine in every aspect of life. By embracing Bhakti Yoga, we align ourselves with the cosmic rhythms and elevate our consciousness, fostering a deep sense of peace and unity with the universe.'

'Stephen', Jim proclaimed, 'your philosophy is not as simple as you make it out to be. Just love God – what does that refer to?'

'Really?' I replied.

Jim continued with a huff: 'Those above words serve as a springboard into a deep philosophical exploration. The phrase suggests a complexity within a seemingly simple directive – "Just love God".

To unpack this, we need to delve into various philosophical, theological and ethical dimensions. At first glance, the directive to "just love God" seems simple and clear-cut. It implies a singular focus on love as the primary or even sole requirement of faith and ethical living. This simplicity can be appealing, suggesting that all complexities of life and moral dilemmas can be resolved through the lens of divine love. However, this approach demands further examination.

'To understand what it means to "just love God", Stephen, we must first define love in this context. Love can be understood in various ways: as an emotion, an action or a state of being. When directed towards God, love often transcends these definitions, encompassing aspects of devotion, obedience, reverence and intimate relationship. In Christian theology, the concept of "agape" is crucial. Agape is a selfless, sacrificial, unconditional love. This type of love is often described as the highest form of love, one that mirrors the love God has for humanity. Therefore, to love God means to embody agape – selfless and sacrificial devotion that seeks not personal gain but the well-being of others and the fulfilment of divine will.

'Different religious traditions have various scriptures that guide their understanding of God and what it means to love Him. For Christians, the Bible is the primary source. For Muslims, the Quran holds this role. Engaging with these texts provides insight into the nature of God and the practical implications of loving Him. Personal religious experiences, such as moments of transcendence, mystical encounters or profound insights, often shape how individuals perceive and love God. These experiences can reinforce one's commitment and understanding of divine love.

'In Islam, loving God (Allah) involves submission to His will, as revealed in the Quran and the Hadith. It is expressed through acts of worship, adherence to Sharia (Islamic law), and striving for moral excellence (*ihsan*). In Hinduism, love for God can take various forms, depending on one's chosen path (yoga). Bhakti yoga, the path of devotion, emphasizes a personal, loving relationship with a particular deity (e.g., Krishna, Shiva). This love is expressed through rituals, prayers and devotional practices. Although Buddhism does not centre on a theistic concept of God, love and compassion are fundamental. Loving-kindness (*metta*) and compassion (*karuna*) are essential practices, aimed at alleviating suffering and fostering spiritual growth.

'In a pluralistic society, loving God also means respecting and understanding the diverse ways others express their love for the divine. This requires an openness to interfaith dialogue, a willingness to learn from others, and a commitment to coexist peacefully. A significant challenge in loving God is maintaining authenticity. How does one ensure that their love for God is genuine and not merely performative or superficial? True love for God must come from a place of sincerity. This means engaging in practices and beliefs not out of obligation or fear, but from a genuine desire to connect with and honour the divine. The balance between internal devotion and external expressions of love is crucial. While rituals, prayers and acts of service are important, they must be rooted in a sincere inner commitment. Jesus criticized the Pharisees for their outward piety that lacks genuine love and humility (Matthew 23:27-28). That's what I understand, Stephen.' Jim gasped, struggling to catch his breath.

Oh boy, I never imagined that in my simple devotion to loving God, an avalanche of complex theories and profound insights would be presented to me in the way that Jim described! It was overwhelming and astonishing to see the depth and intricacy behind my faith, as if a new universe of understanding had suddenly unfolded before me.

'Jim, do you have any understanding of Bhakti Yoga?', I enquired.

Jim paused, a thoughtful expression crossing his face. 'Well', he began slowly, 'a little – all thanks to you. You introduced me to its profound philosophy many years ago, planting a seed of curiosity that has since grown. I've delved into its teachings here and there, exploring the depths of devotion and love that it embodies. I can't claim to be an expert, but I'll see what I can bring to the table.' He looked up, his eyes reflecting a mixture of reverence and enthusiasm. 'Bhakti Yoga is more than just a practice; it's a way of life, isn't it? A path of surrender and unconditional love, connecting the devotee with the divine. It's about seeing the divine in everything and everyone, transforming every action into an act of worship.'

Jim's voice gained a fervent tone, his passion evident. 'It's like a dance of the heart, where the soul's yearning meets the infinite. The stories of the great devotees, their unwavering faith, their pure, selfless love – it's all incredibly inspiring. I may not have all the answers, but I'm eager to dive deeper and share whatever insights I've gathered along the way. Bhakti Yoga, one of the four primary paths of yoga in Hindu philosophy, is centred around the cultivation of love and devotion towards a personal deity or the divine. Deriving its name from the Sanskrit word "Bhakti", which means "devotion" or "love", this form of yoga emphasizes a deep, personal connection with a higher power. It is a path that seeks to transform and purify the practitioner's heart and soul through the power of unwavering love and surrender.

'The roots of Bhakti Yoga can be traced back to ancient Hindu scriptures such as the Vedas and the Upanishads, but it gained significant prominence in the post-Vedic period with texts like the Bhagavad Gita and the Bhagavata Purana. In the Bhagavad Gita, Lord Krishna elucidates the path of Bhakti Yoga to Arjuna, highlighting that devotion to God is a direct and accessible route to spiritual liberation (*moksha*). This is achieved through the complete surrender of the ego and the channelling of all thoughts, emotions and actions towards the divine.

'A fundamental aspect of Bhakti Yoga is its inclusivity and accessibility. Unlike some other paths of yoga, which may require rigorous physical discipline or intellectual pursuit, Bhakti Yoga is open to all, regardless of caste, creed, gender or social status. It democratizes spiritual practice by emphasizing that anyone, through sincere devotion and love, can attain spiritual growth and ultimate union with the divine. The practice of Bhakti Yoga involves several key elements:

'1. *Sat-sang*: This involves associating with like-minded individuals or a community of devotees. *Sat-sang* provides a supportive environment where practitioners can share their experiences, sing devotional songs and collectively enhance their spiritual journey.

'2. *Kirtan* and *Bhajan*: These are devotional songs and hymns that praise the divine. Chanting or singing these hymns with genuine emotion can elevate the practitioner's spirit, creating a sense of unity with the divine.

'3. *Puja* and *Rituals*: Engaging in rituals and offering puja (worship) to deities is another crucial aspect of Bhakti Yoga. These acts symbolize the devotee's love and reverence for God, fostering a deeper connection.

'4. *Japa*: The repetition of divine names or mantras, known as *japa*, helps in focusing the mind and cultivating a sense of divine presence within. This repetitive chanting serves as a form of meditation that brings the practitioner closer to the divine.

'5. Service (*Seva*): Selfless service to others is considered an expression of devotion in Bhakti Yoga. By serving others without any expectation of reward, practitioners purify their hearts and demonstrate their love for the divine in all beings.

'6. Surrender (*Ishvara Pranidhana*): The ultimate aim of Bhakti Yoga is the complete surrender of the self to God. This involves letting go of ego, desires and attachments, trusting in the divine will and accepting all experiences as gifts from the divine.

'Bhakti Yoga is not merely a set of practices but a way of life. It calls for a transformation of the heart, encouraging practitioners to cultivate virtues such as humility, compassion and unconditional love. The stories of renowned bhakti saints like Mirabai, Tulsidas and Chaitanya Mahaprabhu illustrate the profound impact of devotional practice, showcasing how unwavering love for God can transcend worldly sufferings and lead to spiritual enlightenment. In a broader sense, Bhakti Yoga highlights the universal principle that love is the highest form of spiritual expression. By fostering a deep, personal bond with the divine, Bhakti Yoga offers a path to inner peace, joy, and ultimately, liberation.'

Jim continued, his voice deepening with gravity, 'That's it, that's all I can tell you right now about this profound yoga.' The air seemed to thicken with the weight of his words, a sense of mystery lingering.

'Jim', I declared, leaning forward with a mix of admiration and curiosity. 'You're a gold mine of knowledge. Would you share some more of your personal life now with the readers? I'm sure they would be fascinated to learn what you get up to during your rest periods in your realm.'

Jim's eyes twinkled with a secretive glint, and he took one step back, a slow smile spreading across his face. 'Ah, my personal life', he mused, as if unlocking a treasure chest of memories. 'Well, where do I begin? My realm is a place of tranquillity and reflection, where time seems to stand still. When I'm not immersed in the depths of my work, I find solace in the simple pleasures of life.' He paused, his gaze drifting as if seeing distant vistas. 'I spend my mornings walking through lush gardens, the dew-kissed petals whispering secrets of the universe. Each flower, each blade of grass holds a story, a lesson. It's in these moments of quiet contemplation that I find the inspiration and energy to delve deeper into my practices. I would often spend my free time by the crystal-clear lake, its waters mirroring the vast expanse of the sky. I take my small boat out, letting it drift aimlessly – the gentle rocking of the waves lulling me into a meditative state. It's here, amidst the stillness and the soft murmur of nature, that I often have my most profound realizations.'

Jim's voice softened, becoming almost lyrical. 'We can create evenings in my realm if we wish: they are a symphony of colours as the sun sets, casting a golden hue over everything. I gather with wise friends and fellow practitioners, sharing stories, laughter and wisdom by the warmth of the astral plane. These moments of camaraderie are precious, reminding me of the beauty of human connection and the endless quest for knowledge.' He leaned forward, his eyes locking on to mine with an intensity that sent a shiver down my spine. 'Every experience, every moment in my realm is a part of a greater journey, a continuous cycle of learning and growing. It's a place where the mundane meets the mystical, and every breath is a step closer to enlightenment.'

The room seemed to exhale, as if releasing a sigh of quiet awe – the spell of Jim's words gradually dissipating into the air. Each sentence he spoke wove a mesmerizing tapestry, a gateway to the enchanting world that Jim effortlessly inhabited. His life, intricately woven with threads of simplicity and profound wisdom, stood as a testament to the extraordinary beauty nestled within the tapestry of everyday existence.

Jim continued: 'As I mentioned to you a few days ago about this new relationship I've found myself in, each passing moment has deepened my connection with her. Each time I reach out to her, I find myself drawn closer, wrapped in the warmth of her presence.' Jim's excitement grew as he elaborated: 'She took me to see this intriguing new play written by someone completely unfamiliar to me. To my surprise, the performance was utterly captivating! You know how it goes at these plays or operas – every now and then, there's a talent that emerges, destined to become a star in the world of acting or singing. It's incredible to think that I had never even heard of these famous people whom you were fortunate enough to witness firsthand.' His voice carried a mix of admiration and curiosity, reflecting on the missed opportunities and unexpected discoveries that such cultural experiences can bring.

Jim continued with growing enthusiasm, his eyes sparkling with excitement: 'But now I've seen several plays! And not just any plays, mind you, but performances that transcend mere entertainment. I've been fortunate enough to meet a few individuals who are revered in your world – people of immense talent and presence. Recently, we attended a magnificent concert in the park. Picture this: most of our plays and concerts are held outdoors, under a sky that never knows rain. The last concert I attended featured a young woman, a newcomer to our world but already a sensation. Her voice was a marvel, weaving through the air with a grace that enraptured the entire audience. It was not just entertainment; it was an experience – a glimpse into the extraordinary!

'I have been extraordinarily fortunate to find a brief respite from the harrowing battlefield. The calm amidst the storm has granted me moments of peace, a fleeting reprieve from the relentless chaos that defines our existence. Yet, deep within, I am acutely aware that this interlude is but a fleeting breath before I must once again confront the crucible of conflict. The wars that ravage your Earth reverberate far beyond the terrestrial realm, echoing into the very fabric of the astral plane itself. There, amidst realms unseen and dimensions uncharted, battles rage with an intensity that mirrors your own earthly struggles. The ebb and flow of cosmic forces weave a tapestry of strife and upheaval, unyielding to the passage of time or the yearning for respite. As much as I cherish these moments of calm, I know that destiny beckons me back to the front lines. The forces that drive our conflicts, whether mortal or ethereal, show no mercy and grant no reprieve. The mantle of duty weighs heavy upon my shoulders, urging me to return to the fray, to stand once more against the tides of adversity. For in the eternal struggle between light and shadow, peace is but a fleeting illusion. The battles that define us, whether fought in the mortal realm or the ethereal expanse, shape the very essence of our existence. And so, with resolve steeled and spirit fortified, I prepare to heed the call of duty, knowing that the wars of Earth and the astral plane wait for no one. But now I have to go, Stephen', Jim said abruptly, his voice tinged with urgency. 'Chan has contacted me. It seems something important has come up.'

Without waiting for my response, he said farewell and left, leaving me to absorb the sudden silence that filled the room. I watched him leave, a sense of unease settling in my stomach. What could have been so pressing to pull him away so suddenly? Turning back to the desk, I sighed and resumed my task of reviewing the day's writings. The pages were filled with Jim's meticulous notes on Bhakti Yoga, a subject he had become deeply engrossed in over the years. It was fascinating to see how far he'd come since he first entered the spiritual world. His understanding and insights had grown exponentially, reflecting a journey of profound personal and spiritual development.

As I delved deeper into what he'd said, I couldn't help but admire his dedication and the clarity with which he expressed complex ideas. Bhakti Yoga, the path of devotion, seemed to resonate deeply with him, and his passion for it was evident in every word. Each page was a testament to his growth, his struggles and his relentless pursuit of knowledge and enlightenment.

Left alone in the quiet room, surrounded by Jim's thoughts and reflections, I felt a connection not only to him but also to the spiritual journey he had embarked upon. His writings were not just about Bhakti Yoga; they were a window into his soul, revealing the transformation of a man who had dedicated his life to understanding the mysteries of existence.

I closed the notebook, my mind swirling with thoughts of Jim and the unknown urgency that had called him away. Whatever it was, I hoped he would find the answers he sought. As for me, I would continue to explore the depths of his writings, drawing inspiration from his journey as I navigated my own path in the ever-unfolding tapestry of life.

Suddenly my partner entered my office. She looked at me with a sparkle in her eyes, the kind that hinted at an evening of excitement. 'Let's go out for dinner tonight', she suggested with a smile that could light up a room. In that moment, I felt a twinge of guilt, knowing how much she had been looking forward to this. My body was exhausted from a long day, every muscle crying out for rest, but I couldn't allow myself to let her down. Telling her I was too tired would crush her spirit, and that was a line I couldn't cross. So, with a deep breath, I pushed aside my fatigue and matched her enthusiasm with a smile of my own, ready to make the evening special for her, no matter the cost.

A charming Italian restaurant waited for us, its warm glow inviting as I parked the car. We had been enchanted by this place many times before, captivated by its authentic cuisine and cosy ambiance. The memories of laughter and delicious meals shared here beckoned us to return, compelling indulgence in its culinary delights once again. As we stepped out of the car, the enticing aroma of freshly baked bread and simmering sauces filled the air, promising an evening of gastronomic delight and nostalgic comfort. As we settled into our seats, a delightful menu was placed in front of us, brimming with teasing promises of homemade dishes. The tantalizing aromas wafting from the kitchen set the stage for an unforgettable culinary experience.

I began with a starter of Risotto ai Funghi Porcini. The creamy risotto, infused with the rich, earthy flavours of porcini mushrooms and topped with a generous sprinkling of Parmesan, was nothing short of heavenly. My partner opted for her favourite, Calamari Fritti. The lightly fried calamari, perfectly crispy on the outside and tender on the inside, was complemented beautifully by a zesty marinara sauce.

For our main courses, I indulged in Ossobuco. The braised veal shank, cooked to perfection, was served with a vibrant gremolata sauce and accompanied by Risotto Milanese, creating a symphony of flavours and textures that danced on my palate. My partner chose the Branzino al Forno. The oven-baked sea bass, infused with lemon and herbs, was paired with roasted vegetables, offering a delicate yet flavoursome balance that delighted her taste buds.

When it came round for dessert, my decision was easy. I savoured every bite of my usual Tiramisu, a classic Italian delight featuring layers of creamy mascarpone, coffee-soaked ladyfingers, and a dusting of cocoa. Each spoonful transported me to dessert bliss. My partner, content with her meal, decided to skip dessert and opted for a robust coffee instead, enjoying its rich aroma and flavour.

To complement our meal, we chose a bottle of Chianti Classico Reserve. This robust and well-balanced red wine from the Chianti region was the perfect pairing for our Italian feast, enhancing every bite with its deep, complex notes.

Finally, satiated and content, I crawled into bed feeling wonderfully full after such an extraordinary meal-and-wine feast. The evening had been a true celebration of culinary excellence, leaving us both with memories to savour.

11

The Summons

I awoke with a pounding headache, a relentless reminder of last night's overindulgence. My thoughts were muddled – each pulse of pain was a stark echo of the wine that flowed too freely. I groaned inwardly, knowing I couldn't afford to let Jim down. He was counting on me, and despite the agony, duty called. I had to be at my desk, ready to dive into whatever crisis Chan had deemed urgent enough to warrant Jim's abrupt disappearance.

After dragging myself through my morning ritual, each step a Herculean effort, I found some solace in the familiar routine of the kitchen. The kettle whistled and I brewed a strong cup of tea, hoping it would help clear the fog in my head. The scent of toasting bread filled the air, a comforting reminder of simpler times. But the comfort was fleeting. I couldn't shake the sense of unease, the nagging curiosity about what had pulled Jim away so suddenly.

With my tea and toast in hand, I trudged to my desk, every step weighed down by the residual effects of last night's excess. I settled into my chair, the leather creaking beneath me, and took a fortifying sip of tea. The warmth spread through me, offering a brief reprieve from the lingering headache. But as I logged into my computer and opened my emails, a sense of dread settled in. What could Chan possibly want that was so urgent? The screen flickered to life, and I braced myself for whatever awaited.

Just as I finished reading my emails, a sudden, familiar force struck my back, nearly making me drop my tea. The usual hearty slap was followed by Jim's booming, jovial voice echoing through the room: 'Hey there, buddy!'

Startled, I turned to face him, rubbing my shoulder where he had hit me. Jim's grin was wide, his eyes gleaming with mischief as always. My curiosity, which had been simmering, now bubbled over. 'Well', I asked, my voice tinged with impatience, 'what did Chan want?' My heart pounded in anticipation, my eagerness almost tangible in the air.

'It's serious, Stephen. We were summoned to an emergency meeting, a directive issued to all rescuers. An unprecedented and violent incursion has erupted into another sector of the astral plane, a malevolent force storming in from the lower astral realms. This time, however, the assault was meticulously planned, orchestrated by none other than one of the Anti-Christs themselves. Stephen, I don't believe the inhabitants of your world comprehend the true gravity of the situation. Humanity is teetering on the brink of annihilation, far closer to the edge of the abyss than anyone realizes. It's not a gradual decline; it's a reckless sprint toward self-destruction, like lemmings charging blindly toward a fatal cliff. The path humanity treads is perilous, an accelerating descent into chaos and ruin. Every moment, every action, pushes your species closer to the precipice. It's as if an unseen hand is guiding this destructive course, urging humans ever faster toward their own extinction. The urgency of the situation cannot be overstated; the human race is hurtling toward its doom, oblivious to the yawning chasm ahead.'

I was utterly aghast at Jim's words. It was as if a dark veil had been lifted from my eyes, revealing a horrifying reality. When Jim provided me with detailed information on the world's events, it became clear that his warnings were not to be taken lightly.

Jim continued: 'A cataclysmic breakthrough is unfolding in the region known as Palestine. The magnitude of death and destruction inflicted upon its people is beyond comprehension, a nightmarish tableau of human suffering. One of the entities we have long feared, an embodiment of the Anti-Christ, is orchestrating the systematic annihilation of Palestine. The ominous frequency has taken root in that sacred land, a signal that heralds a tide of devastation destined to ripple outwards, engulfing more regions in its wake. The implications are terrifying, and the urgency to act, to comprehend, has never been greater.'

'So', I asked, my voice trembling with curiosity and a hint of fear. 'What's the plan?'

'There are many rescuers involved in that region', he began, his tone grave and eyes shadowed with concern. 'They are doing their best to overcome the lower astrals, but it's no easy task. I've seen the struggle firsthand. The lower astrals are relentless, their darkness thick and suffocating, like a storm cloud that never dissipates. The rescuers are brave, each one fighting with all their might, yet the battle is fierce and unyielding. It's a war not just of strength, but of willpower and spirit. Every moment is a fight to keep the light from being extinguished by the ever-encroaching shadows. Their courage is extraordinary, but the challenges they face are beyond anything you could imagine.'

'Why does God not intercede?', I implored, my voice trembling with the weight of my despair. The silence that followed was deafening – an abyss of unanswered prayers and unfulfilled hopes. My heart pounded against the confines of my chest, each beat a desperate plea for understanding. Again I cried out: 'Why does the Almighty remain indifferent to our suffering?' The raw emotion in my voice echoed through the room, seeking a response that seemed eternally out of reach.

'Stephen, control yourself', Jim began, his tone gentle yet imbued with an otherworldly authority. 'Just because I exist in spirit now does not mean I have all the answers to the mysteries of the universe.' He paused, allowing the weight of his words to sink in, his translucent form shimmering softly.

'What I do know', he continued, his voice growing stronger, resonating with undeniable truth, 'is that a call to God from our heart never goes unanswered.' The room seemed to vibrate with the intensity of his conviction, and I felt an overwhelming sense of peace and hope wash over me. Tears filled my eyes as I whispered, 'Thank you, Jim. Thank you.'

A sip of lukewarm tea settled me down again. I apologized to Jim for my sudden outburst, my emotions having gotten the better of me. 'It's just… just so unfair that so many innocent people must suffer because of those who seek absolute dominance over others.' Jim nodded sympathetically, understanding my frustration. The world seemed increasingly chaotic, with power struggles and conflicts erupting in various corners. I could feel the weight of it pressing down on my shoulders, a relentless reminder of humanity's darker tendencies.

'I get it', Jim said, his voice calm and reassuring. 'Sometimes it feels like we're just spectators to the madness, powerless to do anything.'

I sighed, taking another sip of my tea. The coolness of the liquid contrasted sharply with the heat of my anger, providing a small measure of relief. Spectators, yes, but we're also affected by it. Every decision made by those in power trickles down to us, impacting our lives in ways we often don't realize until it's too late.

Jim stood back, his gaze thoughtful. 'You're right. It's a bitter pill to swallow, knowing that one's fate can be so easily influenced by the whims of a few. But maybe, just maybe, there are ways we can make a difference, even if they seem small.'

His words gave me pause. I had been so consumed by my frustration that I hadn't considered the possibility of making a positive impact, no matter how minor. 'What do you mean?', I asked, genuinely curious.

'Well', Jim began, 'think about it. Every act of kindness, every effort to spread awareness, every time we stand up against injustice – no matter how insignificant it might seem – it all adds up. We might not be able to change the world overnight, but we can certainly influence it in our own ways.'

His perspective was refreshing, a stark contrast to the helplessness I had been feeling. 'I suppose you're right', I said slowly, mulling over his words. 'It's easy to get overwhelmed by the big picture and forget that small actions can collectively make a significant difference.'

Jim smiled, his eyes crinkling at the corners. 'Exactly. It's about doing what we can, where we can. Sometimes, it's the little things that have the most profound impact.'

I nodded, feeling a renewed sense of purpose. It wasn't about being a passive spectator anymore; it was about taking active steps, no matter how small, to contribute to positive change. 'I guess I've been too focused on the negative', I admitted. 'It's time to shift my perspective.'

'That's the spirit', Jim said encouragingly. 'And remember, you're not alone in this. There are countless others who feel the same way and are doing their part to make a difference.'

His words were comforting, a reminder that I was part of a larger community, united by a shared desire for a better world. 'Thanks, Jim', I said sincerely. 'I needed this conversation.'

'Anytime', he replied, his tone warm. 'We're all in this together, after all.'

As I sat there, the tension gradually eased and replaced by a sense of solidarity and determination. The world might be filled with challenges and injustices, but it was also brimming with potential for change. And that potential lay within each of us, waiting to be harnessed and directed towards a brighter future.

With a final sip of my now cold tea, I felt a newfound clarity. It wasn't about the grand gestures or monumental changes; it was about the small, consistent efforts that collectively paved the way for a better tomorrow. And in that moment I realized that perhaps, just perhaps, we all had the power to make a difference, one step at a time.

'Oh yes, before I forget', I asked Jim, 'a friend of mine has asked me to pass a question along to you. Would you answer it for her?'

'I'll try. What's the question?', Jim replied.

'She wants to know if you can provide some information on the Divine Mother aspect.'

'Hmm... I'll have to connect into the library to answer this question', Jim muttered, his voice trailing off into an intense whisper.

His usual chatter faded into an unusual silence, his eyes narrowing and brow furrowing as he focused intently. The atmosphere in the room shifted demonstrably, a heavy stillness replacing the previous lightness. It was as if the very air held its breath, waiting. His fingers twitched slightly, a subtle indication of the mental gears turning furiously within. He seemed to retreat inwardly, connecting with what I could only presume to be a vast, hidden store of knowledge, an enigmatic repository of wisdom and facts.

The seconds ticked by, each one feeling elongated and charged with an almost electric anticipation. I watched, transfixed, as Jim's expression shifted – his eyes growing more intense, his features tightening with concentration. It was as if he was delving into some arcane, secret world, retrieving the answers from the depths of intellectual abyss. The silence was profound, the weight of his focus creating an almost tangible pressure in the room.

Then, without warning, his eyes snapped back into focus, his posture straightening. The moment of profound silence broke, leaving behind an air thick with expectation, and Jim began his understanding of the answer: 'The Divine Mother is the ultimate archetype of maternal love and cosmic creation, an ethereal embodiment of the nurturing essence that weaves through the fabric of the universe. Envisioned in countless forms across various cultures and spiritual traditions, she is the life-giver, the sustainer and the destroyer, embodying the cyclical nature of existence. Her presence is simultaneously gentle and formidable, a paradox of infinite compassion and relentless power. In the vastness of the cosmos, the Divine Mother emerges as a luminous being, her form radiating an iridescent light that transcends human perception. Her visage, a serene amalgamation of beauty and serenity, carries the wisdom of the ages. Her eyes, vast and deep as the ocean, hold the mysteries of creation, time and space. Her embrace is the cradle of the universe, tenderly holding all beings within the folds of her infinite love.

'She manifests in myriad forms, each symbolizing a different aspect of her divine nature. As the nurturing mother, she is Gaia, the Earth Mother, whose bounty sustains life. Her fertile bosom is the source from which all flora and fauna spring, her breath the wind that invigorates all living beings. She is Demeter, whose sorrow and joy dictate the seasons, and Isis, whose magic and compassion transcend the boundaries between life and death. As the fierce protector, she is Kali, the dark mother who dances on the battlefield of existence, her wild hair a halo of liberation and destruction. Her many arms hold the weapons of righteousness, and her tongue lolls out in defiance of all that is unjust. Despite her terrifying visage, her actions are driven by a profound love that seeks to eradicate ignorance and darkness.

'In her celestial form, she is the Virgin Mary, the immaculate vessel of divine grace. Her purity and compassion intercede on behalf of humanity, offering solace and healing to the broken and the weary. She is Kuan Yin, the bodhisattva of mercy, who hears the cries of the world and extends her boundless compassion to all beings, alleviating suffering and guiding souls toward enlightenment. Functionally, the Divine Mother serves as the ultimate source of creation and the eternal nurturer of life. She embodies the principle of Shakti, the primal energy that drives the universe. As the *creatrix*, she gives birth to stars and galaxies, moulds the elements and infuses every particle with the divine spark of consciousness. Her energy is the driving force behind evolution, pushing life towards growth and self-realization.

'The Divine Mother is also the healer, the one who mends the fractured soul and restores balance. In times of despair and turmoil, her presence is a balm, soothing wounds and providing strength. She is the inner voice that whispers wisdom, the intuition that guides us through the labyrinth of existence. Her love is unconditional, embracing all, regardless of their flaws or transgressions. Furthermore, the Divine Mother embodies the principle of transformation. Through her, destruction is not an end but a necessary phase of renewal. Her cycles of creation and dissolution remind us that life is a constant flow, an ever-changing dance of birth, death and rebirth. She teaches us to let go of the old and welcome the new, to trust in the process of metamorphosis.

'In essence, the Divine Mother is the heartbeat of the universe, the eternal source of life, love, and wisdom. She is the sacred ground upon which we stand, the celestial sky that shelters us, and the inner sanctuary where we find peace. Through her, we understand the interconnectedness of all things and the boundless nature of divine love…'

Jim paused, his eyes narrowing as though he had forgotten his words. A deep silence filled the room, stretching out the moment as I watched him with bated breath. But no, Jim's pause was deliberate, a careful gathering of thoughts before he continued with a profound sincerity. He exhaled slowly, the weight of his understanding of the Divine Mother evident in his expression.

'Well, that's it…', he said softly, his voice imbued with a quiet intensity. 'That's what I understand, Stephen. I hope your friend reflects on my words.' Jim leaned forward, his gaze piercing and unwavering. 'Better still', he added, his tone growing more fervent, 'your friend should go into meditation. In the stillness and the silence, she will find what she is looking for herself.'

The air seemed to crackle with the gravity of his message, the room holding its breath, absorbing the depth of his conviction. Jim leaned back, the momentary fervour fading into a serene, knowing smile.

'Thank you, Jim, for your input on the subject. I would like to ask you a question as we are on the subject of meditation. Can you please explain the best method for achieving meditation?'

'No, Stephen, you are well versed in the subject of meditation, you can write on the subject. I'm going to leave you know, and I'll see you tomorrow.'

I decided it was time for a break, so I made myself a cup of tea. As usual, the warmth of the tea was comforting as I took a few moments to relax and clear my mind. After this short interlude, I returned to my desk, eager to delve into the philosophy of meditation as I understood it. I wanted to capture its essence and significance in a way that resonated deeply with me.

Sitting back down at my computer, I began to organize my thoughts and insights into an analogy that would convey the essence of meditation. It was a task that required both clarity and creativity, and I was determined to articulate it in a way that would be both insightful and accessible:

Meditation, a practice with roots stretching back thousands of years, has garnered significant attention in recent decades due to its purported benefits for mental, emotional and physical well-being. Originating in ancient spiritual traditions, meditation has evolved into various forms and techniques, each offering unique pathways to inner peace, mindfulness and personal growth.

To understand meditation fully, I thought further, one must delve into its historical and cultural origins. Ancient texts from Hinduism and Buddhism provide early records of meditative practices aimed at spiritual enlightenment and self-discovery. In Hinduism, meditation (*dhyana*) is a crucial component of spiritual practice, while Buddhism emphasizes mindfulness meditation (*vipassana*) as a means to achieve insight and liberation from suffering.

Across cultures, meditation has found expression in Taoist practices in China, Sufi mysticism in Islam, and Christian contemplative traditions in the West. These diverse cultural contexts have shaped meditation into a multifaceted discipline, adapted to suit different philosophical and religious frameworks.

In recent decades, scientific research has increasingly validated the benefits of meditation on mental and physical health. Studies have shown that regular meditation can reduce stress, lower blood pressure, enhance emotional regulation and improve cognitive function. Neuroscientific research has elucidated how meditation can lead to structural changes in the brain, promoting neuroplasticity and enhancing areas related to attention, empathy and emotional resilience.

Meditation encompasses a broad spectrum of techniques, each with its own objectives and methods. Mindfulness meditation, derived from Buddhist traditions, involves non-judgmental awareness of the present moment. Concentration meditation, such as focused attention on the breath or a mantra, aims to cultivate single-pointed concentration. Loving-kindness meditation fosters feelings of compassion and empathy towards oneself and others, while transcendental meditation utilizes repeated mantra recitation to achieve a state of deep relaxation and heightened awareness.

The benefits of meditation extend beyond relaxation and stress reduction. Regular practise is associated with improved emotional well-being, greater resilience to adversity, enhanced creativity and increased self-awareness. Meditation can also foster healthier interpersonal relationships by promoting empathy and compassion towards others.

For those new to meditation, establishing a consistent practice can be both rewarding and challenging. Setting aside a dedicated time and space for meditation – even if for a few minutes each day – can significantly impact one's well-being over time. Starting with guided meditations or apps that offer structured sessions can help beginners navigate the initial stages of practice.

Despite its numerous benefits, meditation can present challenges, especially for beginners. Common obstacles include restlessness, wandering thoughts and difficulty maintaining focus. Patience and persistence are key to overcoming these challenges, as meditation is fundamentally a practice of returning to the present moment with kindness and without judgment.

Beyond its immediate benefits, meditation serves as a catalyst for personal growth and spiritual development. By cultivating mindfulness and self-awareness, individuals can deepen their understanding of themselves and their relationships with others. Meditation encourages introspection and fosters a sense of inner peace that transcends external circumstances.

Integrating meditation into daily life involves extending its principles of mindfulness and presence beyond formal practice sessions. Mindful eating, walking and listening are examples of incorporating meditation into everyday activities, thereby cultivating a more profound sense of connection to oneself and the world.

In contemporary society, meditation has gained popularity as a tool for stress management and holistic well-being. Mindfulness-based interventions are increasingly integrated into healthcare settings to complement conventional treatments for mental health disorders. Schools and workplaces are also adopting mindfulness programmes to enhance productivity, emotional resilience and overall job satisfaction among employees.

Meditation stands as a timeless practice that offers profound benefits for individuals seeking inner peace, clarity and personal growth. Its rich historical roots, coupled with modern scientific validation, underscore its relevance in today's fast-paced world. By exploring different meditation techniques, understanding its neurological effects and embracing its practical applications, individuals can embark on a transformative journey towards greater well-being and self-discovery.

As soon as I confidently clicked the save button on my computer, signalling the completion of my thoughts on the philosophy of meditation, the tranquillity of my study was abruptly interrupted. With impeccable timing, my partner breezed into the room, her voice carrying a blend of warmth and insistence as she declared that dinner was served and that I should join her immediately.

Her sudden entrance shattered the focused ambiance of my workspace, yet her presence also brought a gentle reminder of the passage of time and the need to reconnect with the world beyond my thoughts. Reluctantly tearing myself away from the glow of the screen, I followed her out of the room, leaving behind the ethereal realm of ideas for the tangible comforts of a shared meal.

12

The Medium of Music

When I awoke to a new day, a startling clarity washed over me like a tidal wave. The vision was vivid, almost prophetic: Jim's story was hurtling towards its inevitable conclusion. Each moment felt like the closing act of a grand play, where every loose end would be tied, every secret unveiled. The air buzzed with a sense of finality, a silent whisper that this chapter of Jim's journey was drawing to a close. But as one story ends, the pages of possibility flutter open. Will there be another book to continue the tale – to delve deeper into the mysteries of Jim's world? The future remains an enigma, wrapped in the fog of uncertainty, waiting to be written.

Soon, I found myself seated behind my desk, anxiously awaiting Jim's voice to signal that he was ready. The screen flickered to life as I booted up the computer, casting a soft glow across the room. Suddenly, the silence was broken by a hearty, booming laughter emanating from behind me. Startled, I spun around to see Jim standing there, his presence revealed through his unmistakable, jovial chuckle. His broad grin and twinkling eyes reflected the contagious energy that always accompanied him, instantly filling the office with a sense of camaraderie and anticipation for the tasks ahead. When Jim asked if I was ready to begin, I turned back to my computer and placed my fingers on the keyboard.

'Stephen', he said, 'I must share with you the astounding beauty of the colours that come alive in my realm through the medium of music. After parting ways with you, I attended a musical recital in the park with a dear friend. It was an experience beyond words. Each instrument, as it struck its note, did not merely produce sound; it conjured vivid hues that danced in the air. The music, already an exquisite auditory delight, transformed into a symphony of colour.

Each note birthed a unique shade, painting the atmosphere in ways I can scarcely describe. The grandeur of the colours accompanying the melodious tunes was a sight that defied my imagination. It was as if the very essence of the music had taken form in an ethereal display of light and colour; it was a spectacle that left me utterly spellbound.

'While I was in the park, I decided to catch up with an old friend, the park keeper who befriended me on my first visit. I wanted my friend to meet him. The park keeper has been in the spirit world for quite some time now. I realized a long time ago that he was not from this plane of existence, but from a much higher one, as his command of astral matter was astonishing. Whenever I wandered through the park, I felt a peculiar connection to him, as if he was guiding me with an unseen hand through the paths and greenery. Yesterday, I found myself drawn to a secluded bench under a towering oak tree. As we sat down, I felt the park keeper's familiar presence beside me, more tangible than usual. We began to converse – not with words, but through thoughts and feelings. His wisdom flowed into me, filling my mind with insights and perspectives that were beyond the understanding of ordinary existence. He spoke of the intricate weave of life and the threads of energy that bind all living things. His knowledge of astral matter allowed him to manipulate the fabric of reality, demonstrating feats that seemed miraculous to the untrained eye.

'He showed us glimpses of his world – a realm of light and harmony – where beings of pure energy moved gracefully through an ethereal landscape. It was a place where time and space were fluid, and the essence of life was understood in its purest form. The park keeper explained that his role was to watch over the park, ensuring that the natural energies remained balanced, so that visitors like us could find peace and solace. As our encounter came to an end, I felt a deep sense of gratitude for the friendship and guidance he had bestowed upon me. The park, once just a place of leisure, had become a sacred ground where I could reconnect with higher realms and gain insights into the mysteries of existence. The park keeper, though no longer of this world, continued to touch my life in profound ways, reminding me of the unseen forces that shape our reality.'

'It sounds so beautiful there, Jim', I remarked. 'The ethereal allure of such a place is undeniable, yet we are inextricably bound by the immutable law of karma. This universal principle dictates that we must fulfil the entirety of our physical existence on the Earth Plane. Our souls are here for a purpose, a divine journey that should not be prematurely interrupted.'

I continued: 'We must steadfastly resist the temptation to end our own lives, no matter how overwhelming the burden may seem. To take one's life, or that of another, outside of the dire necessity imposed by war, would be a grave transgression. When our nation calls us to don its uniform, the act of taking a life is subsumed under the collective karma of the country. In such circumstances, the individual soldier is shielded from the direct karmic consequences of those actions, as the responsibility is borne by the nation as a whole. Thus, we must honour the sanctity of our earthly lives, navigating the trials and tribulations with courage and resilience, trusting that each moment serves a higher purpose in the grand tapestry of our existence.'

'Well, Stephen, it does seem you've grasped the laws of karma quite well', responded Jim. 'Your understanding reflects a deep comprehension of the principle that our actions have consequences, both positive and negative. It's clear you've recognized how our deeds, intentions and even thoughts contribute to shaping our present and future experiences. You've shown an awareness that every action creates a ripple effect, influencing not only our own lives but also the lives of those around us. By acknowledging this, you've demonstrated an appreciation for the interconnectedness of all beings and the importance of making mindful, ethical choices. Your grasp of karma indicates a mature insight into the spiritual and moral dimensions of our existence. Now where was I before I got side tracked?' Jim continued with his narrative: 'I walked briskly away from the park, the laughter and farewells from my friend still echoing in my ears. The spiritual sun was casting long shadows that danced across the ground. I felt a familiar excitement bubbling up inside me; I was about to meet up with my Anna, who had a knack for turning ordinary days into extraordinary adventures. As I approached our usual meeting spot – a cosy little area by the boating lake – I saw Anna waiting there. Her face lit up when she saw me, and she quickly ran over to greet me with a warm hug.

'"Hey, you!" Anna said, her eyes twinkling with mischief. "I've got a surprise for you."

'I raised an eyebrow, intrigued. "Oh? What kind of surprise?"

'Anna grinned and held up two tickets. "We're going to see a play. And not just any play – it's one based on a book by Charlotte Bronte!"

'My eyes widened in surprise. I had always admired Bronte's work, though I had never seen a play that was based on her work performed live. "Really? That sounds amazing!", I admitted .

'Anna beamed. "I thought you'd like it. Come on, we don't want to be late."

'We hurried through the bustling streets. The theatre was a grand old building with a charming, nostalgic aura about it. Inside, the air was filled with a sense of anticipation and excitement. We found our seats just as the lights began to dim. The stage was set with a beautiful backdrop that transported us to a different era. As the curtains rose, I felt a thrill of excitement. The actors and actresses brought the story to life with their powerful performances. Each scene was a masterful blend of emotion and drama, and I found myself completely engrossed in the tale. Anna squeezed my hand from time to time, and I could tell she was just as captivated as I was. When the final curtain fell, the audience erupted into applause. Anna and I joined in, our hands stinging from the enthusiasm of our clapping. As we made our way out of the theatre, we couldn't stop talking about our favourite moments and the incredible talent of the cast.

"That was incredible", I said, still buzzing with excitement. "Thank you for bringing me here."

'Anna smiled and gave me a quick kiss on the cheek. "I knew you'd love it. There's nothing like sharing a wonderful experience with someone you care about", she teased. We walked hand in hand through the city streets, the glow of the theatre still lingering in our hearts. It had been an unforgettable evening, and I felt grateful for the perfect blend of friendship, love and a bit of literary magic.

'In this extraordinary realm, Stephen, the familiar hum of motor vehicles is but a distant memory. Instead, we traverse this land through two remarkable means: either by walking or by the sheer power of our thoughts. Imagine it – merely envision the place you wish to go, and in an instant you find yourself there, as if by magic. This world is replete with destinations to explore, places that echo the comforts and joys you once cherished on Earth. As you wander through this ethereal domain, you'll notice the absence of towering skyscrapers and high-rise offices. The skyline is free from the imposing structures that once defined urban landscapes. Here, the environment is open and unbounded, offering an endless expanse to discover and enjoy. The absence of bustling traffic creates a serene atmosphere, where the tranquillity of nature and the freedom of thought reign supreme.

'Most inhabitants of this realm remain blissfully unaware of the tumultuous events that unfold on the lower planes of existence. Their journey here was serene, having transitioned from their earthly lives in the embrace of natural death. When their time came, they were gently guided by a beloved figure, someone who had departed before, to accompany them to this new, wondrous home. Upon their arrival, these souls find themselves enveloped in an atmosphere of peace and fulfilment. The memories of pain and struggle from their earthly lives fade away, replaced by a profound sense of belonging and tranquillity. They are reunited with those they cherished, able to experience a continuity of love and connection that transcends the bounds of physical existence. In this higher plane, daily life is imbued with a sense of wonder and contentment. Communities are woven together by bonds of mutual respect and affection, and the air is filled with a perpetual sense of joy. Here, the souls engage in pursuits that nourish their spirits and enrich their understanding. They explore vast, picturesque landscapes, partake in communal gatherings, and delve into the arts, sciences and philosophies that ignite their curiosity.

'Time flows differently in this realm – not marked by the ticking of clocks or the changing of seasons, but by the rhythms of our hearts and minds. Each moment is an opportunity for growth and reflection, unburdened by the anxieties and pressures that once weighed heavily upon us. For those who dwell here, the concept of the lower planes – places still fraught with suffering, conflict and the complexities of mortal life – remains a distant, almost abstract notion. The veil between these realms ensures that the serenity of their existence is rarely disturbed. Yet should they choose to look, they can see glimpses of the world they left behind, often with a newfound sense of compassion and understanding. However, most are content to leave that part of their journey behind, focusing instead on the boundless possibilities that lie ahead in this eternal sanctuary.

'Stephen, your world is spiritually bankrupt. Let me explain. This concept reflects not only a decline in traditional religious adherence but also a broader erosion of the moral and ethical foundations that underpin your societies. When we speak of spiritual bankruptcy, we refer to a state where individuals and communities have lost touch with the deeper, intangible aspects of life that provide meaning, direction and purpose. This condition is characterized by a pervasive sense of emptiness and disconnection, despite the material wealth and technological advancements that mark your age. Firstly, let's consider the symptoms of this spiritual malaise. Across the globe, we observe rising levels of anxiety, depression and loneliness. These are not merely medical or psychological issues, but symptoms of a deeper spiritual void. The rapid pace of modern life, with its relentless pursuit of success and material gain, leaves little room for introspection or the nurturing of the soul. Moreover, your societies are increasingly fragmented. The traditional bonds of family, community and faith that once provided a sense of belonging and support have weakened. In their place, you find an over-reliance on social media and virtual connections, which, while useful, often fail to satisfy your deeper need for genuine human connection and understanding.

'The causes of this spiritual decline are manifold. One significant factor is the rampant consumerism that dominates your culture. You are constantly bombarded with messages that equate happiness and success with the acquisition of goods and experiences. This relentless focus on the material not only distracts you from more meaningful pursuits but also fosters a sense of perpetual dissatisfaction.

'Additionally, the secularization of society has played a role. As traditional religious institutions lose their influence, many people struggle to find alternative sources of moral guidance and spiritual fulfilment. While secular humanism and other philosophical frameworks offer valuable insights, they often lack the communal and ritualistic elements that help individuals feel part of something greater than themselves.

'The consequences of spiritual bankruptcy are profound. On an individual level, it manifests as a crisis of meaning, where people find themselves questioning the purpose of their lives. This existential angst can lead to a sense of despair and hopelessness, which in turn fuels destructive behaviours such as substance-abuse and escapism. On a societal level, the erosion of shared values and ethical standards undermines social cohesion. Without a common moral compass, societies struggle to address issues of justice, equity, and sustainability. This fragmentation contributes to political polarization, social unrest and a general decline in the quality of civic life. Despite these challenges, there is hope for spiritual renewal. The first step is recognizing the importance of nurturing your inner lives. This involves making time for reflection, meditation and the exploration of spiritual practices that resonate with you personally. Whether through traditional religious observances, mindfulness practices or other forms of spiritual engagement, we can reconnect with the deeper aspects of our being.

'Furthermore, we must strive to rebuild our communities. This means fostering environments where people can come together to share their experiences, support one another and work towards common goals. Acts of kindness, volunteerism and civic engagement are powerful antidotes to the isolation and fragmentation that plague your societies. Education also plays a crucial role. By incorporating spiritual and ethical development into your educational systems, you can equip future generations with the tools they need to lead meaningful and fulfilling lives. This holistic approach to education emphasizes not just intellectual growth but also emotional and spiritual well-being.

'The world may seem spiritually bankrupt, but this diagnosis is not a death sentence. It is a call to action. By acknowledging the depth of your spiritual crisis and taking steps to address it, you can rediscover the richness and meaning that lie at the heart of the human experience. You should commit to this journey of renewal, both for yourselves and for the generations to come.'

Suddenly, Jim stopped talking, as though he was listening to something or someone. 'Stephen', Jim said nervously, 'I will have to go soon. Chan has just called all rescuers to a meeting. It seems something big is going down on the lower astral plane again.'

My eyes widened at Jim's revelation. The lower astral plane was not a place that people visited on a whim. As we have seen, it is known for its turbulence and the presence of restless spirits – it is a realm where lost souls and negative energies linger. For Chan to call a meeting of all rescuers meant that the situation was dire.

'Do you know what it's about?', I asked, my voice tinged with concern.

Jim shook his head. 'No details yet. Just that we need to be there immediately. It's urgent.'

The room fell silent as the weight of the situation became apparent. Jim's face was tense, and his usually calm demeanour was replaced by obvious anxiety. The lower astral plane was a place of chaos and conflict, a stark contrast to the higher planes of peace and enlightenment. Rescuers like Jim are trained to navigate these treacherous realms, but the unknown nature of the impending crisis added a layer of fear.

I nodded, understanding the gravity of the situation. 'Be careful, Jim. The lower astral plane is dangerous.'

Jim gave a tight-lipped smile, attempting to mask his fear. 'I'll be fine. It's what we trained for, right?' He tried to sound confident, but I could see through the facade. The bond between us allowed for an unspoken understanding; the dangers were real, and the risks were high. Before leaving, Jim turned to me one last time: 'If something happens, if I don't come back…'

'Don't say that', I interrupted, my voice firm. 'You will come back. Just focus on the mission and come back safe. Really Jim!', I said, startled, 'are you not being over dramatic? You and I know that you cannot die?'

With a tremendous laugh Jim nodded, appreciating the encouragement. With one final deep breath he stepped through the portal that linked our realm to the astral planes, his figure shimmering and then fading into the ether. I stood alone in the room, the silence now deafening. I knew the risks the rescuers faced were immense, but I also knew that Jim had been through countless trials before. I had to trust in his abilities and the training he had undergone.

13

The Battle

As the clock struck midnight, I finally succumbed to the heavy pull of sleep. My mind, however, refused to rest, endlessly replaying Jim's haunting words from earlier that day. The rescuers are immortal, yes, but their invincibility doesn't shield them from pain. Each blow lands with cruel precision, leaving a trail of anguish behind.

Jim, my courageous friend, endured countless brutal assaults during the First and Second World Wars, not just on Earth, but also on the treacherous astral plane. He had recounted his harrowing experiences in our first book – *Seven Steps to Eternity* – vivid depictions of a struggle that transcended the physical realm. Though his body was now ethereal, his essence remained painfully human, vulnerable to the horrors he had faced. Can you fathom the terror he endured? From the malevolent beings of the lower astral to the ruthless demons driving their insidious agenda, Jim confronted nightmares that would break the strongest of souls. His spirit may have survived, but the scars of those battles, inflicted by the darkest entities imaginable, linger on, etching an indelible mark upon his very being.

My thoughts were fixated on Jim, and a gnawing curiosity gnashed at the edges of my concentration. This was the second urgent meeting he had been summoned to with Chan, and the sense of unease was profound. 'Well', I mused, trying to quell the rising tide of anxiety, 'I'll soon find out.'

I finished my breakfast – the food turning tasteless as my mind wandered – then headed to my desk. I settled into my chair, every fibre of my being primed and ready, like a coiled spring waiting to be released. The minutes ticked by, each one feeling like an eternity.

Twenty minutes passed, and still there was no sign of Jim. My worry became physical. I felt a tightness in my stomach. Had something happened to him? My mind raced through a litany of possibilities, each more unsettling than the last. The absence of any word from him was an ominous silence that grew louder with every passing second. The usual clatter and hum of the computer seemed distant and muted, overshadowed by the cacophony of my own fears.

I glanced at the clock again, my heart pounding in my chest. Where was he? Had the meeting gone awry? Was he in trouble? The questions swirled in my mind, each one more pressing than the last, creating a maelstrom of dread that I could barely keep at bay. And then, in an earth-shattering moment, a brisk voice sounded out from the ether!

'Sorry, I'm not on time, Stephen. I've only just managed to leave the battlefield on the lower astral plane. The conflict there was far more intense and chaotic than I anticipated. It involved a complex and prolonged struggle that required all my attention and energy to navigate safely. Breaking away from the conflict was incredibly challenging, as I had to ensure I was not followed or affected by any lingering negative energies. Transitioning back to the physical world took longer than usual, which is why I'm delayed. I appreciate your understanding and patience.'

'So, what happened to you when you left me yesterday?', I asked.

'Well, I materialized in the lower astral plane, greeted by an overwhelming sensation of dread. The air was thick with despair, and shadows flickered at the edge of my vision. Chan was there, waiting, along with many other rescuers. Their faces were grim, a reflection of the seriousness of the task ahead. "Thank you all for coming on such short notice", Chan began, his voice steady but grave. "We have detected a significant disturbance here. It's unlike anything we've encountered before. The balance of this realm is at stake, and we need to act swiftly." I listened intently, every word Chan spoke slicing through the tense silence like a knife. My nerves, initially a chaotic whirlpool of anxiety, began to settle into a steely resolve.

'The mission was clear – penetrate the lower astral plane and retrieve the lost souls. The stakes were high, the danger obvious. Chan's voice was calm but grave as he detailed the plan, each step fraught with peril and uncertainty. I felt a surge of adrenaline, knowing this would be one of our most challenging missions yet. But as I looked around at my fellow rescuers – their faces a mix of determination and fear – I drew strength from their presence. We had trained for this, honed our skills, and gathered all the knowledge we could. We were ready, or so I believed. Then, in the midst of Chan's briefing, the reality of our task began to sink in. The lower astral plane was a place shrouded in darkness, teeming with malevolent entities and treacherous traps. Every shadow could conceal a threat, every step could lead us into danger. Yet, we had no choice but to venture into this unknown realm, driven by the hope of saving those who were lost.

'With each word, my confidence wavered slightly, but I clung to the belief that our preparation would see us through. Well, that's what I had thought, Stephen… until now! Now, as we stand on the precipice of the abyss, the weight of the mission bears down on me. The uncertainty is overwhelming, but there is no turning back. We must face whatever awaits us in the shadows of the lower astral plane, for the sake of those we seek to rescue and for our own survival. The real challenge is just beginning.'

'Jim, would you rather discuss something else?', I inquired, sensing that the recent ordeal might still be weighing heavily on his mind.

'No, Stephen', Jim replied firmly. 'Let's press on while it's still vivid.'

'Alright, Jim. But first, a brief pause. I need a drink.'

I stretched my legs and savoured a steaming cup of tea, then returned to my desk, ready to dive back into the conversation.

'Now, where was I?', Jim asked. 'Ah yes – the evil masterminds had set a trap. With malevolent precision, they schemed to divert our resources to the battle raging before us, masking their true, sinister objective: a devastating assault upon the very fabric of the earth plane. These fiends, cunning and ruthless, have entwined themselves with the most powerful people on your planet. Their insidious influence spreads like a dark plague, manipulating leaders, corrupting the noble and bending the will of nations to their malevolent cause. The fate of the world teeters on the edge of a precipice, and time is running out.

'Our enemies, shrouded in darkness and cloaked in deceit, have spent years weaving their web of corruption. They have infiltrated governments, corporations and institutions, embedding their agents in key positions of power and influence. These puppeteers pull the strings from the shadows, ensuring that their machinations go unnoticed by the unsuspecting populace. They have studied humanity's weaknesses, exploiting your greed, your fears and your divisions. Their ultimate goal is not merely conquest but total domination – reshaping the world to fit their twisted vision. The battle we face on the front lines is but a distraction, a smokescreen to keep us occupied while they prepare their final assault. Every skirmish, every confrontation, every casualty we suffer is part of their grand design. They want us to exhaust our resources, to deplete our strength and to sow discord among our ranks. And we have played into their hands, focusing our efforts on the immediate threat without seeing the bigger picture. But now, the truth has come to light. Their veil of secrecy has been pierced, and we stand at the crossroads of destiny. We must act swiftly and decisively, for the hour of reckoning is upon us. The earth plane, the very essence of your world, is their true target. They seek to corrupt it, to bend it to their will, and to unleash a cataclysm that will reshape the world in their image. If they succeed, life as you know it will cease to exist, and a new era of darkness will begin.

'Your task is daunting, but we are not without hope. The courage and resolve of humanity have triumphed over evil before, and you can do so again. You must unite, setting aside your differences and standing together as one. Your strength lies in your diversity, your resilience and your unwavering belief in the light. You must expose the masterminds, disrupt their plans, and reclaim your world from their grasp.

'The path ahead will be fraught with peril. You will face betrayal, deception and unimaginable challenges. But we must press on, guided by the light of truth and the strength of your convictions. Each of you has a role to play in this epic struggle, whether on the battlefield, in the halls of power, or in the hearts and minds of your fellow humans. Remember, you are not alone. Allies, both seen and unseen, stand ready to aid you in this fight. The forces of good are mobilizing – rallying to the cause and preparing to confront the darkness head-on. Together, we will expose the evil masterminds, dismantle their network of corruption and restore balance to the earth plane. The fate of your world hangs in the balance, and the time for action is now! Stand tall, stand firm, and let the light of justice guide you to victory. For you are the defenders of hope, the champions of freedom, and the guardians of the future. Let the battle begin.'

'That's some story, Jim, you must be exhausted after such an encounter. So you faced the lower astrals once again?'

'Yes, Stephen, we did, and what a battle it was. The memory sends shivers down my spine. In one way, I felt a profound sorrow for those poor unfortunate souls whose wills had been completely subjugated by an insidious, malevolent force. You could almost call them "zombies", but even that term falls short of capturing the sheer horror of their plight. They rushed at us with a frenzied fury that surpassed anything you could ever imagine, their eyes devoid of humanity, their movements mechanical yet unnervingly fast. Their screams, a chilling cacophony, echoed through the air – a haunting reminder of their lost humanity. The clash was relentless, a nightmarish ballet of survival and desperation, each moment teetering on the brink of utter chaos. The ground beneath us seemed to tremble under the weight of the confrontation, and for every step we took forward, we were met with a torrent of unyielding, unstoppable rage. It was a battle for our very souls.

'Every breath we took was a struggle; the air thick with the stench of decay and the acrid scent of fear. The sky above us, once a canvas of calm blue, was now an ominous, swirling tempest, reflecting the turmoil below. Our mental weapons seemed almost useless against the sheer numbers that assailed us, a ceaseless wave of bodies driven by a dark, unholy energy. Their faces, twisted and contorted, bore no resemblance to the people they once were. It was as if we were fighting shadows of the damned, caught in a purgatorial loop of violence and despair.

'Amidst the chaos, there were moments when time seemed to stretch, each second an eternity of horror. The sounds of battle were a symphony of terror – clashing steel, desperate cries and the relentless, guttural moans of the soulless attackers. Our comrades fell around us, one by one, but soon they got back up once again and re-entered the fight, their sacrifices a grim testament to the ferocity of the onslaught. Blood stained the earth, of the dead soldiers who watched this battle happening right in front of them – a stark reminder of the price they paid for every inch of ground we held. In those harrowing hours, I saw bravery and terror in equal measure. I witnessed acts of selfless heroism and moments of utter despair. The bond forged in the crucible of that battle was unbreakable; a shared experience of horror and hope that will forever bind us together. The enemy was relentless, their onslaught a tidal wave of malice, but we stood our ground, driven by a determination that transcended fear. And when the dust finally settled, and the last of the cursed fell, we stood victorious but not unscarred… The battlefield was a grim tableau of death and destruction, a silent testament to the hell we had endured. Yet amidst the ruins and the bodies of the newly fallen, there was a flicker of hope – a reminder that even in the darkest of times the human spirit can endure and prevail.

'Stephen, it's time I took a rest. I've heard you had a visitation from another interesting soul recently. Am I correct? Perhaps you could share the details of this encounter with your readers. It sounds like there might be quite the story behind it?'

With those words, Jim left, leaving an air of mystery behind him. I had not encountered the person he referred to previously. The episode Jim mentioned took place just the other evening. I was sitting by the computer, ready to write that week's blog, when something extraordinary happened. What follows is the account of that night, and this is that blog:

As I sat at my computer, my mind leisurely meandering through potential topics for this week's blog, I was abruptly interrupted by a most commanding presence. It was a robust male voice, resonant with a certain distinguished air, that spoke directly to me. Startled yet intrigued, I discerned that this was no ordinary visitor, but rather a spirit of considerable character and bearing. With a touch of playful levity, he declared: 'I have a message for your readers.'

I inquired of his name. He responded with a dismissive wave of his hand. 'Names are merely destinations', he said, his voice resonating with a timbre of deep-seated wisdom and experience. 'It is what I bring to the table that truly counts. When I walked the Earth many years ago, I wore many hats. I was a healer of bodies, a doctor who delved into the intricacies of human frailty and resilience. I was an editor, shaping the written word with precision and care, guiding others to find their voices. I was also a writer of fiction – novels – weaving tales that transported readers to realms of imagination and introspection. Each role was a chapter in the grand narrative of my existence.

'Now, in this ethereal realm I have embraced a new role: a messenger of words. I convey truths that transcend time and space, whispering wisdom into the hearts of those willing to listen. My purpose is not defined by a name, but by the legacy of knowledge and inspiration I leave in my wake.' He paused, his eyes reflecting a universe of untold stories and unspoken truths. 'Names', he continued, 'are simply markers on the path. It is the journey and the contributions we make along the way that define us.'

He caught me by surprise, but I found his rhetoric quite amusing, and asked if he would not mind continuing.

'Not at all, old boy' – and so he continued: 'In the mists of time, from the realms beyond mortal comprehension, a voice emerges. It is the voice of the spirit world, a chorus of ancient wisdom and ethereal insight, seeking to illuminate the shadows cast by the machinations of the living.

'In the hallowed halls of eternity, where the echoes of the past intermingle with the dreams of the future, we spirits gather in sorrowful contemplation. From this vantage, unburdened by the constraints of time and place, we observe the unfolding tableau of human ambition and folly. The winds of war once again whisper through the corridors of power. The land of Ukraine, Israel and many more countries are places of rich history and resilient spirit, standing as a crucible in the forging of new conflicts. We see the hands of the West, draped in the shrouds of righteous intent, moving pieces on a grand chessboard, each manoeuvre cloaked in the language of freedom and defence. Yet from beyond the veil, we perceive the deeper currents, the ancient cycles of power and dominion, masked by the façade of noble cause. The spectre of a third great war looms, its shadows lengthening with each provocation, each strategic alliance and each echoing threat. Why, oh mortals, do you persist in this endless dance of destruction? Have the lessons of the past been so readily forgotten? We who dwell in the aftermath of countless wars, weep for the suffering that could be averted, the lives that could be spared. The spirits of those lost in previous conflicts call out, their voices a haunting reminder of the price paid for the hubris of nations. We see the sorrow of the mothers, the anguish of the fathers, the dreams extinguished before their time. In the halls of eternity, these sorrows are etched into the very fabric of our existence. Each tear shed in the mortal realm reverberates through our ethereal home, a poignant reminder of the fragility of peace and the ever-present spectre of conflict.

'Beware, ye who wield the power of the living, for the path you tread is fraught with peril. The fires you kindle may consume more than your intended adversaries; they may engulf the world you seek to protect. The seeds of discord sown today may bloom into a harvest of unparalleled devastation. From our vantage, we see the possibilities branching out like an ancient oak. There are paths where diplomacy prevails, where understanding bridges the chasm of mistrust, where humanity rises above its baser instincts to embrace a future of collective prosperity. These paths are fraught with challenges, yet they are illuminated by the light of hope and the promise of peace.

'Listen to the whispers of the past, to the voices of those who have walked this earth before you. Heed their warnings, learn from their mistakes. The power to change the course of history lies not in the machinery of war, but in the hearts and minds of those who dare to envision a different future. The echoes of ancient conflicts resound through time, carrying with them lessons unheeded and sacrifices unrecognized. Each generation inherits the legacy of those who came before, yet too often, the hard-won wisdom of the past is cast aside in the fervour of present ambitions.

'The spirit world is a repository of human experience, a silent witness to the cycles of creation and destruction that define mortal existence. From the vantage point of eternity, we see the folly in the pursuit of power for its own sake. The boundaries drawn on maps, the alliances forged in secrecy, the rhetoric of nationalism – all these are but fleeting constructs in the grand tapestry of time. They are shadows on the wall, ephemeral and insubstantial, yet capable of casting long and devastating shadows across the lives of millions.

'In our realm, the souls of the departed dwell in contemplation of their earthly lives. They carry with them the weight of their actions, the consequences of their choices. Those who have waged war, who have sown the seeds of conflict, who have sacrificed the lives of others for their own gain, find no respite in the afterlife. Their spirits are burdened with the knowledge of the suffering they have wrought, and they yearn for redemption that can only be found in the actions of the living.

'We, the spirits, have seen the horrors of war in ways that the living can scarcely imagine. We have witnessed the devastation of entire civilizations, the erasure of cultures, the obliteration of human potential. We have seen the suffering of innocents, the anguish of those caught in the crossfire, the despair of those who have lost everything. In the face of such suffering, the justifications of power and politics ring hollow. Yet despite the darkness, we also see the glimmers of light that persist in the human spirit. We see the capacity for compassion, the strength of community, the resilience of hope. It is these qualities that have the power to transcend the cycles of conflict and create a world where peace is not merely a fleeting respite between wars, but a lasting foundation for human flourishing. Thus, we implore you, the living, to heed our counsel. Turn away from the path of war and destruction. Seek instead the path of understanding, of dialogue, of mutual respect. Embrace the diversity of the human family, recognizing that our differences are not a source of division, but a wellspring of strength. In the unity of purpose, in the shared commitment to the common good, lies the potential to overcome even the greatest of challenges.

'The conflict in Ukraine is but one manifestation of the broader struggles that beset humanity. It is a flashpoint in a larger narrative of power and resistance, of domination and defiance. But it is also an opportunity – a chance to break the cycle of violence and to forge a new path forward. It is a call to action for the leaders of the world, for the people of all nations, to rise above the narrow interests of state and to embrace the universal principles of justice and peace. In the silence of eternity, we spirits watch and wait. We hold our breath, hoping against hope that the living will find the wisdom to choose a different course. For in the choices made today lie the seeds of the future – a future that can be shaped by the light of reason and compassion, or darkened by the shadows of conflict and despair. Remember, mortals, that the power to shape the future lies in your hands. Each action, each decision, ripples through the fabric of time, creating patterns that will endure long after you have passed from this world. Choose wisely, and let the legacy you leave be one of peace, of understanding, of hope. Thus, from the silence of eternity, we implore you: Seek not the path of war, but the path of understanding. For in that choice lies the salvation of all.'

'Whoa', I blurted out. 'That was a monologue!'

'I suppose it was', the entity replied with a slight laugh.

Before I could even open my mouth to ask if he would reappear when needed, he vanished in the blink of an eye, leaving nothing but a whisper of his presence behind. I sat there, stunned and speechless. 'Well', I thought, 'can you beat that?!' The abruptness of his departure was as mysterious as his sudden arrival, and I was left grappling with the enigma of his fleeting visit.

The day had been fraught with harsh realities, and I was forced to come to terms with several of them. From the moment I woke up, I could sense an impending weight that would follow me through each hour of the day. There were financial concerns gnawing at the back of my mind, personal relationships that seemed to be fraying at the edges, and a lingering feeling of self-doubt that coloured everything I did. Each of these issues demanded my attention, pulling me in different directions and leaving me feeling as if I was stretched very thin.

Facing one's own limitations and vulnerabilities is never an easy task. It's a journey that requires more than just a moment of contemplation; it demands a deep dive into the aspects of ourselves that we often prefer to ignore. The realization that I couldn't fix everything overnight – or perhaps at all – was a bitter pill to swallow. It required a level of introspection that made me confront uncomfortable truths about my own inadequacies and the areas in my life where I had fallen short.

As the day progressed, I found myself oscillating between feelings of frustration and fleeting moments of clarity. It was in these moments that I began to understand that acceptance doesn't equate to defeat. Instead, it means acknowledging where I am right now and understanding that it's okay to have limitations.

This realization was both daunting and liberating. It freed me from the unrealistic expectations I had placed upon myself and allowed me to see the path forward more clearly.

By evening, as I sat quietly with my thoughts, there was a sense of peace that began to settle. The day's events had not changed, and the challenges still lay ahead of me, but my perspective had shifted. Accepting my vulnerabilities didn't make me weaker; it made me more human – more connected to the shared experience of struggle and growth that we all go through. In that acceptance, I found a new strength to face the next day with a little more courage and understanding.

14

Chan's Gift to Jim

The morning sunlight streamed through the gap in the curtains, casting a warm glow over the room. I stirred beneath the covers, feeling the pull of the day ahead. With a reluctant sigh, I pushed myself up, swinging my legs over the edge of the bed. The cool floor beneath my feet sent a shiver up my spine, jolting me into full wakefulness.

I shuffled to the bathroom, still rubbing the sleep from my eyes. The mirror reflected a familiar, albeit groggy, face. Turning the faucet, I let the water run until it was steaming hot, then stepped into the shower. The cascade of warm water was like a gentle embrace, washing away the remnants of sleep and the fog of dreams. I closed my eyes, savouring the sensation as the water flowed over me, revitalizing every muscle.

After what felt like both an eternity and a fleeting moment, I turned off the water and stepped out, wrapping myself in a soft, fluffy towel. I dried off quickly and dressed in comfortable clothes, ready for a day of creativity and productivity. The scent of freshly brewed coffee greeted me as I made my way to the kitchen. The rich aroma was invigorating, a promise of the energy I needed to start the day. I poured myself a cup – the dark liquid steaming, invitingly. On the counter, a simple but satisfying breakfast awaited: toast with butter and a side of fresh fruit. I ate quickly, enjoying the quiet solitude of the morning.

With my hunger sated and my mind alert, I moved to my desk. My computer sat waiting, the screen dark and silent. I powered it on, watching as it came to life. The familiar hum of the machine was a comforting sound, a signal that the day's work was about to begin. I settled into my chair, adjusting my posture for maximum comfort. My fingers hovered over the keyboard for a moment, and then I took a deep breath, ready to begin. As I waited for Jim to make his appearance, I read through his words from yesterday. I felt a sense of excitement and anticipation. His words were always a source of strength and a guiding light that helped shape my own thoughts and ideas. I smiled, ready to dive into the tasks he would outline, confident that today would be a day of progress and creativity.

With a final sip of my coffee, I began to type, the words flowing effortlessly from my mind to the screen. The day had only just begun, but already it was filled with promise. Suddenly, the room was engulfed in the intoxicating scent of roses, as if a garden had materialized out of thin air. Through the fragrant haze, Jim's voice rang out, filled with laughter and warmth. 'These are for you, Stephen', he exclaimed joyfully, as he gently placed a stunning bunch of 'astral roses' on my desk.

I was struck speechless, my senses overwhelmed by the unexpected beauty and the gesture of friendship. The astral roses, with their ethereal petals shimmering with hues of celestial blue and soft lavender, seemed to glow softly in the ambient light of the room. Each bloom carried a delicate fragrance that whispered of distant galaxies and precious secrets.

I looked up at Jim, my heart overflowing with gratitude and wonder. His eyes sparkled with mischief and kindness and his smile was wide and infectious. In that moment, amidst the roses and the shared laughter, I realized the depth of our friendship and the beauty of unexpected gestures that can brighten even the dullest of days. But soon I would come down with a bump.

'Look' – he remarked, a flicker of uncertainty crossing his face before he continued – 'our friendship isn't exactly the type where I regularly bring you flowers. These, well, they're actually a gift from my girlfriend. You see, I've been telling her about you – about your unwavering commitment, your relentless pursuit of excellence – and she felt these flowers would be a heartfelt thank-you for all the support you've given me.' His words carried a touch of apology, as if he feared his actions might be misunderstood. Yet there was sincerity in his eyes as he spoke, a genuine desire to convey gratitude and recognition for the efforts that had undoubtedly strengthened our bond.

'They're not just any flowers', he added, a hint of warmth softening his tone. 'She specifically chose them because she knows how much your hard work means to me. They're a symbol of appreciation, a gesture from both of us to acknowledge everything you do.' Oddly enough, Jim seemed to expect that I would grasp the sentiment hidden behind it all – that gratitude sometimes manifests itself in the most unexpected yet sincere ways. However, instead of a heartfelt moment, I found myself struggling to stifle uncontrollable laughter. It was one of those times where the humour caught me off guard, and try as I might, I couldn't stop chuckling for several minutes. Jim, bless him, couldn't help but join in the hilarity of the situation. Eventually, after what felt like an eternity of shared laughter, Jim reluctantly switched back to his usual commanding demeanour.

'When I left you yesterday, Chan and I and a few others decided it was time to rejuvenate our energies. With a serene resolve, we made our way to the pool of eternal strength accompanied by Chan, my trusted spiritual guide. As we approached the shimmering waters, a sense of peace enveloped me. We all immersed ourselves, feeling the cleansing power of the pool wash over us, renewing our spirit and fortifying our aura. Chan stood beside me, offering quiet encouragement and wisdom, his presence a testament to the bond between mentor and mentee, united in the pursuit of spiritual growth and inner harmony.

'The area surrounding the pool is a veritable paradise of lush flora, creating a sensory feast with its vibrant colours and intoxicating fragrances. The air is perfumed with the sweet scent of myriad flowers, each bloom contributing its unique perfume to the atmosphere. Towering trees stand sentinel, their canopies offering dappled shade that dances on the water's surface. Among them, clusters of vibrant tropical flowers burst forth in a riot of hues: vivid reds, oranges, pinks and purples that contrast beautifully against the verdant greenery. The ground is carpeted with a tapestry of emerald grass and delicate ground cover, interspersed with small, fragrant herbs that release their aromatic oils with each step. Butterflies and bees flit from bloom to bloom, adding to the lively hum of the natural symphony. As the day progresses, the changing angles of sunlight create a dynamic play of light and shadow, enhancing the beauty of this natural oasis. The overall effect is one of tranquillity and harmony, where the pool is not just a centre-piece but part of a larger, breathtaking tapestry of nature's bounty.

'As we lounged around the shimmering pool, basking in the warmth of this plane, I seized the moment to broach a subject I had often asked about but never received an answer. With a casual tone, I turned to Chan, catching his gaze as he adjusted to my words. "Chan", I began tentatively, my voice carrying a weight of curiosity tinged with a hint of apprehension, "how long have you been in the spirit world?" The question hung in the air, pregnant with unspoken mysteries that had long intrigued our circle of friends.

'I knew the answer I expected, having posed this question countless times before. Chan was an enigma wrapped in layers of secrecy, his past veiled in shadows deeper than the pool. Each time I ventured into the territory of his previous life, it felt like pushing against an invisible barrier, unsure if I would provoke a storm of resistance or unlock the floodgates of revelation. He regarded me with a calm yet inscrutable gaze, his eyes betraying nothing of the tumult within. The gentle lapping of water against the pool's edge provided a soothing backdrop to the intensity of our exchange. For a fleeting moment, the world seemed to hold its breath, waiting for his response.

'"You already know the answer to that", he replied softly, his voice carrying a depth that belied its quiet timbre. There was a pause, pregnant with unspoken truths and unexplored dimensions of existence. "Some things are better left to the currents of time."

'His words hung in the air, mingling with the scent of the flowers and the distant hum of cicadas in the summer heat. It was a gentle rebuff, delivered with a grace that softened the edge of my persistent curiosity. In that moment, I realized that perhaps understanding Chan's journey required more than just questions; it demanded a patience and respect for the boundaries he chose to uphold. And so, as we sat in silence, the conversation shifted like ripples on the water's surface, leaving the enigma of Chan's spirit world experiences to linger in the quiet spaces between our shared stories and unspoken histories.

'"Now, Jim", Chan instructed with a commanding tone, his voice echoing through the room. "Repeat your question again?" I found myself momentarily struck dumb. Could it be that he was finally ready to unveil his deepest secrets to us? I knew I was treading on delicate ground. Chan was notorious for his reluctance to discuss his previous life, and prying too much could easily sour the relaxed atmosphere we were enjoying. Yet curiosity gnawed at me, fuelled by the mysterious aura that surrounded him. Chan chuckled softly, his eyes scanning the water's edge before meeting mine with a faint smile. "You're not giving up on that question, are you?" I shrugged nonchalantly, masking my eagerness behind a sip of chilled water. "Just curious, that's all. You've always kept us guessing." His expression softened, a hint of contemplation crossing his features. "Maybe one day, I'll surprise you all", he replied cryptically, his voice tinged with a touch of nostalgia. "That day has arrived!"

'I was utterly stunned by his words, feeling a rush of disbelief and confusion. My heart pounded as I tried to comprehend the gravity of the moment. "You mean now – you're going to reveal your true being to us?" My voice trembled, a mix of fear and anticipation lingering. The air seemed to close in around us. My eyes were fixed on him, waiting for the revelation that would change everything we thought we knew. I was utterly stunned by his words, feeling a rush of disbelief and confusion. My heart pounded as I tried to comprehend the gravity of the moment.

"'Yes, I took the name Chen and turned it into Chan, but my birth name is Hanshan Deqing. I was also known as Chan Master Hanshan. I was a highly esteemed figure in Chinese Buddhism during the late Ming dynasty. I was born in 1546 – my original name was Chen Deqing, and my journey into the profound depths of Chan (Zen) Buddhism began at an early age. I later became renowned for my deep spiritual insights and reformative efforts within the monastic community. As Hanshan Deqing, I was born into a scholarly family, which provided me with a solid foundation in Confucian education. However, from an early age, I was drawn to the spiritual path. At the age of nine, I began studying Buddhism and by fifteen, I had already taken my vows as a novice monk. My commitment to the monastic life and my rigorous practice earned me recognition, and I was fully ordained at the age of eighteen. My early years in the monastery were marked by intense study and meditation. I was particularly influenced by the teachings of the Lankavatara Sutra, which emphasizes the mind-only doctrine and the nature of consciousness. My profound understanding of these teachings set me apart from my peers and laid the groundwork for later contributions to Chan Buddhism.

"'One of the pivotal moments in my life came during my studies at the renowned Nanhua Monastery. There, I delved deeply into the works of the Sixth Patriarch, Huineng, whose teachings on sudden enlightenment and the inherent Buddha-nature of all beings had a lasting impact on me. My interpretation of these teachings was both profound and practical, emphasizing direct experience over theoretical knowledge. Perhaps I am best known for my efforts to reform monastic practices and revitalize Chan Buddhism during a time of decline. I saw that many monastic communities were becoming lax in their discipline and that the true spirit of Chan was being lost amid rote rituals and scholasticism. In response, I advocated for a return to rigorous meditation practice and a focus on the direct experience of enlightenment. My teachings were characterized by their simplicity and directness. I often emphasized the importance of meditation in daily life and the need to remain mindful and present in every moment. I believed that enlightenment was not a distant goal but something that was accessible to anyone who sincerely practised.

"'My influence extended beyond my immediate disciples. I wrote extensively, and my works, including commentaries on key Buddhist texts and my own treatises, have been studied by generations of practitioners. My writings are noted for their clarity and practical advice, making them valuable resources for those on the Chan path. In addition to spiritual teachings, I was also involved in social welfare activities. I believed that the principles of Buddhism should extend to all aspects of life, including helping those in need. My compassionate actions and commitment to social justice earned me widespread respect and admiration.

"'I passed away in 1623, but my legacy endures. I am remembered as a reformer who breathed new life into Chan Buddhism and as a compassionate teacher who guided countless individuals on their spiritual journeys. My life and teachings continue to inspire practitioners around the world, embodying the timeless wisdom of the Chan tradition. In summary, my life was a testament to the transformative power of dedicated practice and compassionate action. Through my reforms, teachings and writings, I left an indelible mark on Chinese Buddhism, ensuring that the essence of Chan would continue to thrive for generations to come. Now you know who I am, are you satisfied?", Chan asked with a dry smile across his face.

'We were all utterly stunned by Chan's revelation about his life. None of us, least of all me, had any inkling of his true identity. The air was thick with shock and silence as we processed his words. I felt my throat tighten, my mind racing to grasp the enormity of his confession. It took several long, agonizing minutes before I could finally find my voice: "Thank you for sharing", I managed to say, my voice barely above a whisper. One by one, the rest of the group echoed my sentiments, each expression of gratitude tinged with awe and disbelief. We all knew that in that moment, everything had changed irrevocably.

'After our exhilarating dip in the pool, where Chan's unexpected revelation sent shockwaves through our group, I felt an electrifying surge of energy coursing through me. The intensity of the moment lingered, leaving me both breathless and invigorated. As the sun held its place, painting the sky in hues of orange and pink, and with my mind buzzing with the day's events, I decided to part ways with Chan and my friends. Determined to share this newfound vitality, I sought out my girlfriend. We spent an unforgettable time together – our laughter echoing through the air, each moment more vibrant and alive than the last. And now, I find myself here with you, ready to embrace whatever adventures lie ahead.

'As I reach the conclusion of this ethereal journey we have shared, it is with a mix of gratitude and a touch of melancholy that I bid you farewell. For the past few weeks, our connection has bridged the realms of the living and the spirit world, allowing me to impart the essence of my experiences and insights. This collaboration has been a testament to the profound bond that can exist between souls, transcending the boundaries of life and death. From the moment we first connected, I felt a sense of purpose and clarity. The task of recounting my journey in the spiritual world was not one I took lightly. Each moment, each memory, and each revelation was shared with the intent of offering you, and those who read these words, a glimpse into a realm that often eludes the understanding of those still anchored in the physical world. In the beginning, I was but a whisper in the wind, a fleeting presence seeking a voice. You, with your open heart and receptive mind, became that voice. Through you, I was able to articulate the wonders and mysteries of the afterlife, a world that is as real and vibrant as the one you inhabit, yet infinitely more profound.

'I have shared with you the serenity and beauty of the spirit world, a place where love and light reign supreme. Here, souls are free from the burdens and struggles that often define earthly existence. We exist in a state of perpetual harmony, where the essence of our being is unencumbered by physical limitations. It is a place where we are reunited with loved ones who have passed before us, where the bonds of love are strengthened and renewed. Yet it is also a place of growth and learning. In the spiritual world, we continue to evolve, guided by the wisdom of those who have ascended to higher planes of existence. We are given the opportunity to reflect on our earthly lives, to understand the lessons we learned and to prepare for future journeys. It is a realm where forgiveness and understanding prevail, where we come to terms with the choices we made and the paths we walked. I have recounted my encounters with other souls, each one a unique and beautiful expression of the divine. From the joyous reunions with family and friends to the profound connections with spiritual guides and mentors, every interaction has deepened my understanding of the interconnectedness of all life. We are all threads in the vast tapestry of existence, each one contributing to the greater whole. Through our connection, I have also shared the challenges and trials of the spiritual world. While it is a place of peace and enlightenment, it is not without its difficulties. There are moments of introspection and reckoning, times when we must confront the shadows of our past and the consequences of our actions. But these moments are not to be feared; they are opportunities for growth and transformation. In facing our fears and accepting our flaws, we become more fully realized beings, capable of greater love and compassion.

'As our time together draws to a close, I want to express my deepest gratitude to you. Your willingness to open yourself to my presence and to serve as a conduit for my words has been a gift beyond measure. Through you, I have been able to fulfil a sacred duty, to share the wisdom and beauty of the spirit world with those who seek understanding and solace. It is my hope that the words we have shared will continue to resonate with you and with all who read them. May they offer comfort to those who mourn, guidance to those who seek, and inspiration to those who strive to live lives of love and compassion. Remember that the spirit world is always near – a realm of infinite possibilities and boundless love – waiting to welcome each soul when the time comes.

'As I prepare to withdraw from this connection, Stephen, know that my presence will remain with you in spirit. The bond we have formed is eternal, a testament to the enduring nature of love and the interconnectedness of all souls. Whenever you seek guidance or solace, know that you can reach out and I will be there – a whisper in the wind, a flicker of light in the darkness. I've also delved into the mysterious and perilous depths of the lower astral plane, where shadows whisper and darkness lingers. It is a realm fraught with danger, where the air vibrates with the echoes of lost souls and malevolent spirits. My work there is not for the faint of heart, for I confront the most sinister forces that thrive in the crevices of human fear and sorrow. In this ethereal battleground, I wage an unending war against the shadows that seek to engulf your world.

'Every encounter is a test of will and courage, as I navigate through the spectral mists and confront entities born of pure malevolence. Their eyes glow with a darkness that seeks to pierce the very essence of my being, yet I stand resolute, wielding the light of truth and hope. The battles are fierce, and the scars they leave are not always visible to the naked eye, but they are etched into the fabric of my soul. And so, my work will persist as long as evil festers in the hearts of men. As long as there are those who succumb to the lure of darkness, I will be there, a beacon of light in the abyss. The struggle is eternal, but my resolve is unwavering. For in every victory, no matter how small, lies the promise of a brighter dawn, a world where shadows fear to tread.

'Farewell, dear friend. May your journey be filled with light and love, and may you continue to be a beacon of hope and understanding in a world that often yearns for both. Until we meet again in the boundless expanse of the spirit world, know that you are cherished and loved.'

This farewell message encapsulates the profound experiences and lessons shared between me and the spirit of Jim, offering a heartfelt conclusion to the journey we've undertaken together.

Jim certainly can be called a Ghost Writer!

Books to challenge your perception of reality

A message from Clairview

We are an independent publishing company with a focus on cutting-edge, non-fiction books. Our innovative list covers current affairs and politics, health, the arts, history, science and spirituality. But regardless of subject, our books have a common link: they all question conventional thinking, dogmas and received wisdom.

Despite being a small company, our list features some big names, such as Booker Prize winner Ben Okri, literary giant Gore Vidal, world leader Mikhail Gorbachev, modern artist Joseph Beuys and natural childbirth pioneer Michel Odent.

So, check out our full catalogue online at
www.clairviewbooks.com
and join our emailing list for news on new titles.

office@clairviewbooks.com

CLAIRVIEW